Clinker Boatbuilding

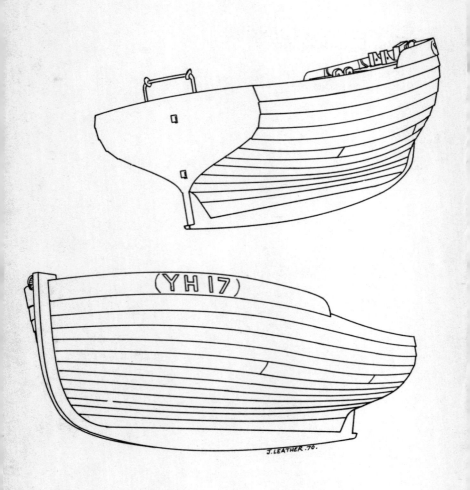

(YH 17)

J. LEATHER .70.

John Leather

Clinker Boatbuilding

Drawings by the author

ADLARD COLES
8 Grafton Street, London W1

Adlard Coles
William Collins Sons & Co. Ltd
8 Grafton Street, London W1X 3LA

First published in Great Britain in hardback by
Adlard Coles 1973
Reprinted 1974,1976,1977,1980
Paperback edition 1987
Reprinted 1988, 1990

Distributed in the United States of America
by Sheridan House, Inc.

British Library Cataloguing in Publication Data

Leather, John
 Clinker boatbuilding
 1. Boatbuilding – Amateurs' manuals
 2. Clinker boats – Design and construction
 I. Title
 623.8'202   VM321

 ISBN 0-229-11818-6

Printed and bound in Great Britain by
Richard Clay Ltd, Bungay, Suffolk

Contents

Illustrations

Introduction

This book describes clinker and cold-moulded construction methods for building small boats up to 20 ft length, of modern or traditional form, for sailing, rowing or power propulsion. It is intended to fulfil the needs of anyone, anywhere, wishing to build a small boat; and approaches the subject step by step, in simple terms and with many diagrams.

The term 'clinker' planking is used throughout the book in preference to the older English 'clencher' and 'clench-built', or the American 'lapstrake'.

Building a small clinker or cold-moulded boat offers a rewarding challenge, which increasing numbers of people are undertaking to satisfy a desire to create a useful craft which may also be of superior workmanship. This gives a sense of satisfaction in building which is unobtainable with boats constructed from kits or built from glass reinforced plastic.

The painstaking amateur can build a superior wooden boat if he makes the effort. The materials cost is small and he has a big advantage over the professional boatbuilder in that his time costs nothing and he can afford to lavish it on his creation. There are already thousands of enthusiasts in America building their own seaworthy and individual clinker planked small craft, and recreational boatbuilding is growing in that country, where the term 'hand crafted' means great pride in ownership and individuality which can only be achieved expensively by now almost nonexistent professional labour or pleasurably with the use of simple hand tools and inexpensive materials. This movement is spreading in Britain and Europe, and has always existed strongly in Australia and New Zealand.

Reinforced plastic has become an increasingly common material for small boats and there are hundreds of dinghy types on the market throughout the world, but almost all the sailing dinghies are designed for racing or have been developed with the characteristics of racing craft. Even the so-called 'family' dinghies need an athletic crew in anything more than a gentle breeze. Most of them also have limited stability and carrying capacity for numbers of adults, children and their gear.

Plastic general purpose boats have brought boating to the masses, but the nature of the construction and its cost has required that their design be as versatile as possible, and they are usually compromises in sailing or rowing characteristics, convenience for outboard power and light weight for trailing behind a car. Many boat owners desire one of these qualities before the others and a great many like a boat to have individuality and give pride of craftsmanship—something the mass-produced boat can never achieve. Many need small, general purpose sailing and rowing boats of light, strong construction which are stable for safe, family use, satisfying to own, can be sailed by one person if necessary, yet are well proportioned and sail well.

So, paradoxically, the widespread use of plastic as a boat-building material, and increasing leisure, have combined to stimulate the desire of many to build a small wooden boat at home. This is not pure reaction or sentiment but an expression of individuality by people who prefer a really superior boat suited to their own needs. Often it stems from ownership of a larger plastic craft which needs little maintainence. The owner misses the opportunity to 'tiffle about' with the boat, which is part of the pleasure of owning a wooden craft, and turns to building himself a dinghy for rowing or odd use; perhaps as tender to the larger craft which may yet give him greater pride of ownership. More pleasure can usually be had from a knock-about dinghy than from an expensive cruiser; a fact recognised by many of the distinguished names in yachting.

The decision may be one of aesthetics. For many the well built wooden boat of superior traditional design is a thing of beauty, quite apart from her functional utility, and her creation is as satisfying as possession, particularly if of a rare or perfected type. For the 'one off' home built boat, or for an owner with discriminating taste, wood will remain the best material for cheapness, simplicity and satisfying enjoyment of construction.

Marine modelling is another growing form of relaxation in craftsmanship, and model makers will find much to interest and aid them in this book. A well built clinker boat model on a scale of perhaps $\frac{1}{12}$ or $\frac{1}{16}$ full size is a rewarding task, almost equivalant to constructing the actual boat. Examples such as a gig, a beach lugger, ships' boats of various periods, or a sailing dinghy will provide hours of fascinating construction, conveniently carried out in the home. It might also be advantageous for the amateur boatbuilder to construct a scale model as an inexpensive trial for his projected full sized boat.

This book is a practical handbook, not a history, but the long story of clinker boatbuilding is part of its continuing fascination. It is among the oldest forms of boat construction, popularly associated with ancient Norse longships and sailing dinghies, but it was also widely used for 2000 years to build many large craft, from Hanseatic cargo ships to Tudor warships and nineteenth century sailing coasters and paddle tugs. Principally used in Western Europe, Scandinavia and North America, it also appeared in scattered places elswhere.

Much seafaring history has been made in clinker boats; a clench-built Norse longship probably made the first voyage of discovery to North America, and centuries later clinker-built ships' boats first ran the keels of the western world on beaches of remote continents and islands. Clinker boats went on hazardous cutting-out expeditions, made hopeless ocean voyages with storm-battered survivors, or formed the myriad types of tough, subtly salty, beach fishing boats which beat out through the surf by tens of thousands in the days of sail and are still developing in the age of power.

By the eighteenth century, development of clinker lightness and strength made it desirable construction for fast sailing craft. Cutters carried fleet despatches home from famous or disastrous actions, their roaring wake matched by the stealthy speed of a big smuggling lugger pursued by an equally large, clench-built cutter of His Majesty's revenue service. The Falmouth packets tumbled across Atlantic seas to bring news of the troubled American colonies, staggering under pyramids of sail rivalling the fruit cutters standing home from Spain with cases of fragrant oranges chocked off in the holds for the London market.

Clinker boatbuilding spread with colonisation to North America, Australia, New Zealand, the Cape and to many other parts of the world where white men settled. For generations the

American emigrants' farewell was the English pilot dropping into his clinker-built boarding boat to return to the cruising cutter, and the first contact with the new world was the lapstrake yawl boat pulling alongside from the lee of the Sandy Hook pilot schooner, perhaps 300 miles from the American coast. English and Scandinavian emigrants built clinker boats from native woods and in eastern America 'lapstrake' construction, as it became renamed, was widespread; from the tough utility of open spritsail boats hauling trawl lines off No Mans Land to the elegant lightness of the Rangely Lake guide boats.

Clinker boats gradually took many forms: exaggeratedly overcanvassed racing skiffs in Sydney harbour; a cargo wherry whispering through the reedy Norfolk channels; Deal luggers or Dunkirk lamaneurs beating out through a Channel gale; top-hatted ship chandlers in stylish Whitehall boats rowing among Boston's shipping; Seabright skiffs powering out to the fishing grounds through the roaring New Jersey surf; beamy Koster boats standing out into the stormy Kattegat; pram dinghies of Norwegian sealers hauled up on the Arctic ice; Cape Town mullet boats winging like seabirds under spritsails; uncompromisingly bold Yorkshire cobles; bluff Aldeburgh beach boats; lean Clyde lugsail skiffs; incredible labour aboard a herring lugger; exuberant speed in a Suffolk beach yawl.

The men who built most of these boats were skilled craftsmen backed by generations of tradition and experience, but there were many thousands of others, fishermen, farmers and waterside dwellers who, needing a small craft for their livelihood, had to build as best they could. Only simple hand tools were available and they had never studied drafting or boat design, while very few indeed were able to lay off lines. Yet these men built seaworthy and often ingenious and beautiful small boats. Today's amateur, with advantages of education and modern tools, can take heart from this example.

The traditional clinker boatbuilder had a simple procedure in his skilled craft and the use of plans was a late development. Keel, stem and transom were made and assembled upright on stocks at convenient working height. Bevels and rebates were cut as necessary and a midship section mould or shadow mould might be prepared. After a final check with level and plumbob, and with everything shored and braced, the boat was ready to plank. This was done largely by eye, from the garboard upwards, working the planks in pairs so that both sides were planked with equal pressure and were clenched as the planks were fitted. When planking was completed the bent frames, or in many cases sawn frames, were fitted, followed by the gunwales, risings, thwarts, knees, floors and other finishing items.

Clinker boatbuilding developed as a skilled trade, reaching perfection in the superbly formed gigs, dinghies and sailing cutters of the big yachts and developing the workmanship of the golden-varnished sailing dinghies which flourished in hundreds of one-design classes throughout the world. It survives professionally, but is rapidly becoming a handcraft of relaxation.

An amateur will almost certainly build from plans for convenience, and his first attempt could well be a pram dinghy, as the simple shape, with transoms at bow and stern, is more easily planked than the stem dinghy. The stem shape demands more skill and allied to a shaped tuck stern offers a worthwhile challenge to craftsmanship of which the builder will be proud.

The sequence for building a small clinker planked boat as described in this book may be briefly summarised as follows:

Preparing a building site, tools and materials
Laying off the full size hull lines and construction details
Making moulds and templates
Setting up building stocks
Making and erecting the keel, hog, stem, apron, deadwoods, sternpost, centreplate case and transom
Erecting the moulds
Marking out plank edges
Spiling planks
Fitting or hanging planks and clenching land nails
Making and fitting bent timbers
Clenching timber nails
Fitting gunwales, risings, thwarts, knees, breasthooks and rowlock chocks
Fitting floors, if required
Fitting deck beams and deck planking if required

Fitting floorboards, cleats and chafing bands to stem and keel

Making and hanging rudder

Making mast and spars and fitting ironwork

Painting and varnishing

Stepping mast and setting up rigging

Bending sails

Receiving the compliments of other boatowners

In contrast to the centuries-old clinker boatbuilding tradition, cold-moulding is the latest serious development in wooden boatbuilding, enabling the professional or amateur to mould craft of the most intricate shape and superb finish, simply and economically, from layers of thin timber bonded by waterproof adhesives.

Cold moulding has been used to build the finest yachts and the smallest dinghies equally well. For lightness with strength it is unequalled, and gives pleasure in creating a hull which has the traditional feel of wood combined with the ability to be stored out of the water or in the sun and wind for long periods without opening up.

Cold moulding has been developed for 30 years in Britain and deserves to be better known to builders elswhere, who will find it wood's answer to the best qualities of glass reinforced plastic. It is the wood boatbuilding method of the future.

1 Building Preparation, Materials, Fastenings and Glues

Preparation

Most amateurs are capable of building a wooden boat of construction and finish comparing well to a professionally built boat, providing they make thorough preparation.

Tools

Sharpening tools is the first thing a boatbuilder must know or learn by practice, and it is time well spent, particularly with planes and chisels. Much boat construction consists of accurate fitting of curved surfaces, and a really sharp tool used with only average skill will leave a curved or straight surface which has no irregularities and will fay (fit) to another. A blunt tool will stick and score, making the surface which results from much labour impossible to fit to anything, and may damage the item beyond rectification. Blunt or inefficiently set saws will bind, splitting and spoiling the planking; blunt planes and spokeshaves will tear the grain, particularly with elm or African mahogany; blunt drills will break off short in awkward places where they are difficult to extricate.

Comparatively few hand tools are necessary to construct a well built boat. Their cost is reasonable and once purchased they are useful assets. Builders' requirements differ widely; some produce good work with few tools, making good deficiencies by ingenious use of what they have. The following list is intended as a guide to essentials. It would be possible to dispense with some items or to substitute others. All can be obtained from a good tool supplier.

A good panel saw, 20 in. long, 10 teeth per in., with a narrow blade, if possible. The teeth should be fine with not too much set, i.e. not bent or set alternately very wide apart from each other.

Rip saw, 28 in. long, 6—8 teeth per in.

Tenon back saw, 10 in. long, blade about $3\frac{1}{2}$ in. wide.

Turning or compass saw, narrow in the blade for cutting sharp curves.

Saw files for sharpening.

Saw set, for setting or adjusting the angle of saw teeth.

Trying plane, wood or steel. A long plane for trueing long straight timber.

Jack plane, wood or steel. A steel plane is more easily kept sharp but a wood plane is lighter to use.

Smoothing plane, wood or steel, 3 in.

Plough plane, $\frac{1}{2}$ in.

Rebate plane, $\frac{3}{4}$ in.

Spokeshave, large. Steel, with adjustable iron.

Broad chisel, $1\frac{1}{2}$ in.

Chisel, 1 in.

Chisel, $\frac{1}{2}$ in.

Mortice chisel, $\frac{3}{4}$ in.

Mortice chisel, $\frac{1}{2}$ in.

Gouge, flat curve, $1\frac{1}{4}$ in.

Gouge, half round, $\frac{5}{8}$ in.

Hammer, $1\frac{1}{2}$ lbs weight.

Wood mallet.

Ratchet brace. With set of twist bits from $\frac{1}{8}$ in. to $\frac{1}{2}$ in. diameter; a countersink bit, and $\frac{3}{4}$ and 1 in. centre bits.

Twist bit, $\frac{5}{8}$ in. For boring rowlock holes.

Bradawl.

Screwdriver, large with $\frac{1}{2}$ in. blade.

Screwdriver, small.

Flat steel file.

Flat wood rasp, 8 in.

Round wood rasp. 8 in.

Pair pinchers.

Pair nail cutters or nippers.

Wood rule. 2 ft type.

Square.

Plumbob and string.

Ajustable marking bevel.

Chalkline and reel.

Shifting gauge for marking wood.

Pair of steel dividers with screw setting.
Spirit level, as long as can be afforded.
Oilstone.
Six in number, 6 in. steel cramps.
Bench vice, woodwork type.
Bench vice, ironwork type.
Two wood sawing stools (sometimes called sawing horses).

The following tools would need to be made by an amateur but are part of the normal equipment of a professional boatbuilder. Occasionally they can be bought or borrowed.

A clenching hammer of about 6 oz. weight is desirable, with a thin, almost flexible handle. A good clenching hammer must have a long, narrow head as it balances better than a short-headed hammer of equal weight. Such hammers cannot often be bought but a light cabinetmaker's hammer may be found which has these characteristics. A suitable hammer can be made from a piece of $\frac{1}{2}$ in. diameter steel rod, $3\frac{3}{4}$ in. long. One end is squared and ground to a slight convex shape. The other is ground to the ball end of a ball-peen hammer. At the centre the head is drilled at right angles to take an oak or hickory handle. The hole should be slightly elongated to give room for the handle without weakening the head. The head need not be hardened as steel is much harder than the soft copper nails.

1   Rooving iron or burr set

Rooving iron, used to drive the rooves or copper washers onto the nails to be riveted or clenched (1). The larger end of the tool is also used to hold against the head of the nail when clenching or turning it. A rooving iron can also be made from a $\frac{1}{2}$ in. diameter steel rod about 4 in. long with a $\frac{3}{16}$ in. diameter hole drilled lengthwise down its centre for about 2 in. from one end.

3

Six wooden wedging cramps, or nippers (2). The wedges may be of oak or ash, fastened to the cramps with string to save time spent hunting for lost ones. The faces of the wedges should be smooth and flat so they will set up easily with pressure from the hand.

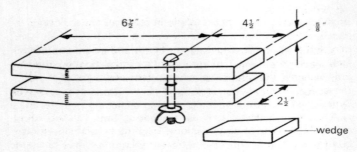

2   Wedging clamp or nipper

A batten for lining out planking and checking fairness is essential. This must have a uniform rectangular section and be slightly longer than the boat under construction. Typical dimensions for small boatbuilding are $\frac{3}{8}$ in. thick by $1\frac{3}{4}$ in. wide. A clear-grained, knot-free pine is the best wood. Choose something close-grained and springy which will bend evenly throughout its length, yet is soft enough to take nails without splitting. The edges must be square and accurate so that whichever way it is bent a fair curve or sweep is obtained. When not used battens should be laid flat and straight, preferably on a rack where air can reach all sides evenly, to avoid warping. If the necessary length of batten is unobtainable, two pieces may be scarphed and glued together from timber of slightly larger size than the finished batten. When the glue is set, one edge of the batten is planed true against a straightedge and is entered in a circular saw bench with the fence open to a fraction under the rough width of the batten, which is run through a fine toothed saw. The saw fence is then closed in and the batten is turned and run through for the other edge, repeating this process a few times until the desired measurement of perhaps $1\frac{3}{4}$ in. is achieved. The batten is then turned on end and run through in a similar way for thickness. Finally the batten 'off saw' is very carefully planed to finish true on all faces.

Building preparation

Boats can be and are successfully built in the open, but this is usually inconvenient and should be avoided if possible. Sun, rain and frost are injurious to the work and bad weather will stop construction. Lack of light reduces hours of work, and the time wasted in collecting and returning tools will often make the builder reluctant to work for the odd hour in the evenings which can soon advance construction.

A sound shed, outbuilding or empty room is the most desirable building place and should be large enough to take the boat and a bench. This will reduce building time and make it possible to achieve a good finish. Boats are often built in premises having earth floors, but a strong wooden floor assists setting up the boat and keeping the shop clean. Good light and sufficient working room are essential. A minimum is 4 ft longer than the boat to be built and 4 ft wider than the boat's maximum breadth, plus the width of the bench. It might be possible to manage with a little less length but it is almost impossible to have less width as a man cannot bend, stoop, strike with a hammer or use a brace or drill in the same space within which he can merely stand.

It should be possible to use elementary steaming facilities for bending timbers, either inside the building space or adjacent to it, and the effect of clenching noise on any neighbours should be considered. Means of removal of the completed craft should be carefully checked, if these are difficult, by making a batten mock-up of the boat's principal overall dimensions and carrying it out to test the exit.

Many amateur builders prefer to erect a temporary building in the garden and typically this might be framed up with 2 in. by 2 in. fir, in pairs of uprights 5 ft apart, with a header along the top of the same size. Plain roof trusses of a double slope with horizontal tie beam and a vertical kingpost, all of 2 in. by 2 in., should be fitted above the posts. The roof trusses should be covered by longitudinal purlins of $1\frac{1}{2}$ in. by $\frac{3}{4}$ in. battens nailed at 12 in. intervals from the ridge. A few raking braces of the same material will make the framework rigid and it can then be covered with heavy grade, clear polythene sheeting, making it wind and rain proof yet giving excellent light. A second-hand door could be fitted for access.

In many urban and other areas there are probably local planning restrictions on such a temporary building and a call at the local authority offices will be worthwile. Permission should be readily granted for a period sufficient to construct a small boat.

The building premises should be equipped with a bench which should be as long as possible. A minimum size would be 6 ft long and 2 ft wide. Sometimes it is possible to borrow a carpenter's bench from a house builder. Alternatively, two 9 in. by $2\frac{1}{2}$ in. planks, equal in length to the boat to be built, can be securely fastened horizontally to one wall at a height of not more than 2 ft 9 in. or lower than 2 ft 3 in., for an average person's use. Tools should preferably be hung on the walls from battened racks rather than being crammed in a toolbox or littering the bench. All timber to be used in construction should be neatly stacked, blocked up off the floor and laid level to avoid warping and distortion.

The floor and every part of a boatbuilding shop should be kept reasonably free of shavings to avoid waste of time locating dropped nails, screws and tools; besides diminishing the risk of fire from accidentally dropped cigarettes or matches.

Stocks

The foundation on which a small wooden craft is built is called the stocks. The type and arrangement of stocks will depend on whether the boat is to be built right way up or upside down. Professional builders of clinker boats prefer to build right way up and this is also better for amateurs. If a clench-built boat is built upside down, fitting of the garboard and lower strakes is easier, but the remaining planking is more difficult and may result in a poorly shaped sheer to the topside planks, which would mar the boat's appearance and the amateur builder's pride. Building upside down also means that the boat would have to be removed from the moulds when planking is completed and turned over for fitting the bent timbers. As the structure is not very rigid at that stage there is risk of straining it and losing the true shape.

Apart from these aspects, it is not so easy to judge if the sheer is correct when the boat is upside down, despite careful and accurate work, and it usually needs a little correction to obtain a fair line; possibly the most aesthetically important line in the hull. Also, as the boat when planked is only half built, if she is turned over she must again be firmly supported so that the remainder of the work can be done efficiently and comfortably. In boats with a rockered keel bent to shape instead of sawn, it is difficult to keep this curve from altering; the keel tries to spring up, away from the moulds, as the planking is fitted and to shore against this down onto the moulds requires them to be very strongly made. Also, when the boat is built upright the builder can reach over the top of each strake as it is fitted, to clench the plank land fastenings from the inside, while his other hand presses the dolly against the nail heads on the outside. In this manner one man can easily manage the land fastenings.

Thus, most advantages are with the upright method of building as the boat, once set up, is not moved until completed and the various shores and struts are removed gradually as work progresses.

The usual arrangements of stocks for upright building (3) consist of a rigid plank, slightly longer than the boat, supported firmly and well stayed, with the upper edge planed true and straight. The methods of supporting it vary. Two trestles may be used if well fastened down, though trestle legs get in the way of feet. For convienient working the plank should be raised so that its top edge is about 21 in. above the floor, which allows easier boring of fastenings in the garboards and working on the keel rebate. A 9 in. by 3 in. pine plank makes a good stock if planed and set up level. When the keel is placed on the stocks it is held wedged in position by small double wedges between wood cleats which are screwed to the stocks (4). These cleats must be kept below the lower face of the garboard strake. With a rockered keel they will be set higher at the ends than amidships, and it is best to fix these after the boat is set up. With a

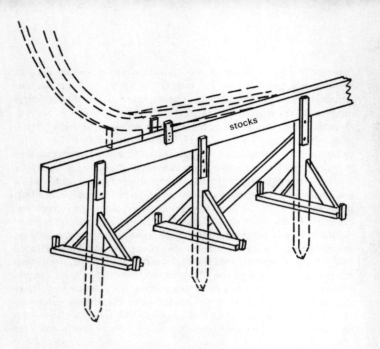

4 Keel wedging on stocks

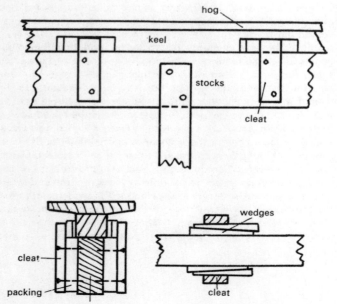

centreboard boat, where the keel width is swelled out in way of the centreboard case it is necessary to fit a packing piece between the cleats and the stock. In upright building the moulds will be stayed at the top, and unless the roof or ceiling has rafters showing, it is an advantage to set up vertical posts at the ends of the stocks and fit a stiff plank or rooftree between them, to which braces can be nailed. This may not be necessary if the stem and transom are well fixed.

If working in a confined space with a door at one side only, the stocks should be arranged to allow a plank to be passed over or under them from one side to the other; an important point in setting up.

Stocks are sometimes set up, without a horizontal member (5). The posts are driven into the ground, braced as shown and cut off at the appropriate heights to support the keel. The heights are measured from a stretched line forming a datum. The top of each post is usually notched to receive the keel. This is an inferior arrangement to that with a horizontal stock, but is still sometimes used in primitive conditions, and was once used to build large craft (5a).

For building in an inverted position uprights of about $2\frac{1}{2}$ in. by $2\frac{1}{2}$ in. are suitable for small boat work and are either driven firmly into the ground or cleated to the floor (6). The tops of these are lined up and bevelled. At the sides of the top of the stocks boards of about 6 in. by 1 in. section, planed true on the top edges, are temporarily nailed to the stocks and levelled. The height to the upper edge of these boards should be at least 18 in. to permit access to the inside of the hull from below.

The 'ladder' method of mould erection may be used instead of stocks. This ensures a fair shape and an easy method of positioning the moulds, besides holding them rigid and permitting fastening the garboards without interference from posts or braces. For the ladder, two 2 in. by 4 in. section pieces of wood are required, long enough to extend about 15 in. beyond the length of the boat. These must be perfectly straight, otherwise setting up will be inaccurate. The ladder sides are laid side to side on edge, on the floor or bench, and the mould spacing from the lines plan is measured and marked on them, being squared across both pieces. The sides of the ladder are spaced about 2 ft or 2 ft 6 in. apart, depending on the beam of the boat, and

9

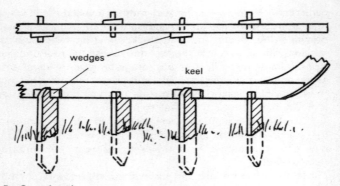

wedges

keel

5 Ground stocks

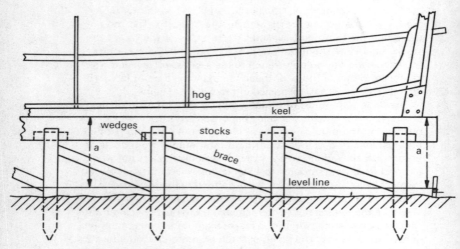

hog

keel

wedges

stocks

brace

a

a

level line

5a An alternative form of ground stocks

must be exactly parallel. Cross cleats of 4 in. by $1\frac{1}{4}$ in. section are prepared and are screwed on at the mould stations exactly at the squared lines. The ends of the cleats must not protrude beyond the sides of the ladder and the ends must be squared. When assembled, the sides of the ladder and the cross cleats must be at right angles and form accurate location for the moulds which will be rigidly fastened to them.

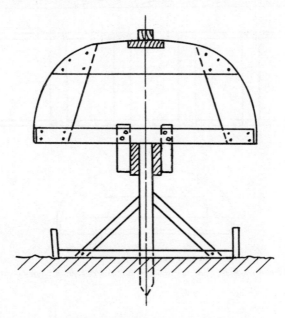

6   Stocks for building in an inverted position

To locate the moulds vertically at their correct relative heights they are made with extensions which raise them the correct distance above the ladder. The various lengths making these extensions are determined from a line added to the profile view of the lines plan. It corresponds to the top of the ladder and is laid off parallel to the baseline from which the height offsets are measured. The moulds are all made to extend to this line and are screw-fastened to the cross cleats (7a and 7b).

11

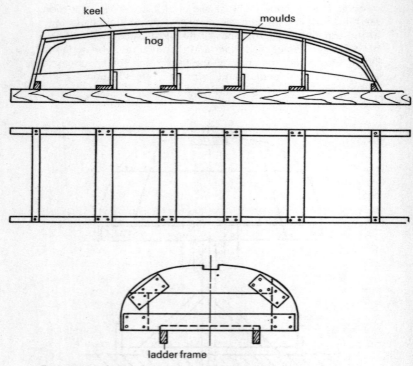

keel

moulds

hog

ladder frame

7a, b Ladder method of erecting moulds. Building of a pram dinghy illustrated

The hog, keel, stem, transom and sternpost can be erected on the moulds, additional cross cleats being fitted as necessary to take the stem and transom. When the moulds and centreline structure are erected on the ladder the moulds must be checked with a batten for fairness as described for conventional setting up. Before planking can commence the assembly must be turned over so the hull will be planked right way up and at a convenient working height. One method is for the extended

12

ends of the ladder sides to be supported on stools of equal height, screw-fastened to the ladder and the floor. Alternatively, four corner posts may be fitted at the ends of the ladder sides, or one end of the ladder can be screw-fastened to cleats nailed to a wall, the other end being supported as described.

Timber

Wood for boatbuilding should always be felled in the winter while the sap is low, as this reduces the possibility of rot. Only the best possible timber should be used to build a boat and it should be carefully selected to suit the part of the structure to be made from it. If a boat is to be built from a designer's plans, these should specify the timbers in detail. However, it is now often necessary to substitute alternative timber to that specified.

Some difficulty may be found in obtaining suitable boatbuilding timber in small quantities. The ordinary timber merchant or builder's sawmills do not usually stock timber suitable for boatbuilding, and a large timber yard often cannot be bothered with a comparatively small order. If the builder has some experience of timber he can of course select it personally. If not it is best to attempt to buy from a timber yard which has been, or still is, a supplier to professional boatbuilders. An alternative might be to approach a professional boatbuilder to go with you to select the timber, for which service he would be paid a fee covering use of his time and knowledge. If this is not possible and the timber merchants have no experience of supplying timber for boatbuilding, it would be best to request the assistance of the yard foreman, to whom it should be emphasised that only the best straight-grained, clear timber is of use. His selection may be checked with these notes. Correct selection of timber in tree trunk form (in the round) or in baulks, requires much experience and expert advice should be sought. It may be necessary to buy different woods from various merchants, as some specialise in hardwoods, some in softwoods and others in native grown timbers or imported woods.

The amateur boatbuilder may find difficulty in the confusion of names given to timbers within the timber trade, particularly to softwoods, which have so many closely related types; and indiscriminate use of the terms 'fir' and 'deal' cause confusion. The number of timbers covered by the misleading term 'African mahogany' are often named from the districts where they are cut or shipped, and a single variety will often vary much in quality.

Good timber, when struck with a hammer, should give a clear ringing sound. A dull sound usually indicates shakes or decay. The ends of stacked planks, boards or flitches should be examined and those with the grain running straight with the edges at the ends may be marked for further 'culling' or examination. Those showing the heart should be rejected.

The colour of the timber should be even, allowance being made for the difference between the heartwood and sapwood. Scattered areas of irregular colour usually mean incipient rot.

If to be used for planking or other longitudinal members, the timber should be straightgrained and as free from knots as can be obtained. Spruce and larch, which are both good for planking small craft, usually cannot be obtained without knots, but where these occur they should not be 'dead' or black.

Decay in softwoods is often indicated by grey colour. In oak it is shown by pink areas and in elm by places lighter than the surrounding timber and more yellow in shade. Star shakes at the ends of boards are not serious unless deep and air cracks at

8   Heart shake in timber

the ends do not usually penetrate far and are not damaging A heart shake is the defect which should be carefully looked for and is usually found in boards containing the heart of the tree (8).

A board with the grain running to a tongue, particularly possible in spruce, should be discarded as when sawn into thin planking, dried and under bending strain the tongue will develop into a long shake which cannot be remedied.

Timber is sold at a price per cubic foot in the size being offered, or it may be priced at 'per foot super, as inch' (per inch of thickness) from which its price in any size can be calculated by adding the cost of sawing to reduce it to the required size. A small additional charge is usually made for selected quality timber, but is worth paying to a reliable merchant.

Sawing to any required size is charged per foot of area sawn. If a board or plank is sawn down its thickness to make two thinner planks it is termed 'cutting', but if sawn through the face of the board it is termed 'ripping' and the charge is made per foot super.

If the length of timber to be cut is greater than the pur-chaser's requirements the waste has usually to be paid for and taken.

In sawing timber there is a loss in thickness taken by the saw kerf of a least $\frac{1}{8}$ in. If the planking is bought in, say, 3 in. thick pieces of suitable length and width to allow for the shape of the planks and is cut into $\frac{3}{8}$ in. finished thickness planed boards, four cuts will produce five boards of a total thickness of 3 in. less four $\frac{1}{8}$ in. sawcuts. Therefore each board, off the saw, will be $\frac{1}{2}$ in. bare and after planing on each side will finish at $\frac{3}{8}$ in. thick.

Planking bought planed from the sawmill is usually rather rough and the planks generally require finishing with a sharp, fine-set hand plane before they are nailed in place.

Boards for planking should not be less than about 12 in. wide, if possible, as the shape of the planking is impossible to determine accurately before planking the hull commences; it is often necessary to cut a 4 in. width plank from a board 10 in. or more in width to obtain the true developed shape.

If it is necessary to scarph some planks to achieve the desired length it is best to arrange to cut one wide plank and one narrow one from the same board to minimise waste. Some of the offcuts from the planking may be used later in items such as bottom boards.

To obtain the quantity for ordering planking the longest strake should be scaled from the waterlines on the half breadth plan, but as the strake may be longer, because of the amount of sheer, than is apparent from the plan, it is best to add 9 in. to the scaled dimension. The quantity for ordering, in super feet, is this length in feet multiplied by the girth at the quarter length, measured from the sections on the body plan from sheer to sheer, plus 50 per cent allowance for waste. This is obviously not an exact figure but in practice will be found efficient. It is best not to underestimate as it is sometimes necessary to reject a plank and any waste can be used for other items. If the builder runs short it may be difficult to get the small additional quantity to finish the job.

Ideally, timber for boatbuilding should have an air-dried moisture content of not more than about 20 per cent and should be stored in the driest possible conditions. This is often difficult for amateur builders, who usually have to stack timber out of doors, but if it is covered by waterproof sheets it should remain reasonably dry. It must always be remembered that thousands of small wooden craft have been satisfactorily built throughout the ages in the most primitive conditions and with elementary wood storage facilities, by men who had no knowledge of the exact moisture content except that the timber was dry, wet, or too wet to use. Moisture content is very important if timber is to be glued, when it should be around 15 per cent and the timber must be kept in dry storage.

It is recommended that all timber used in construction be brush-treated with a wood preservative before the boat is painted. There are various types of preservative of which Cuprinol is probably the best known. However, a very reliable and inexpensive traditional mixture was one part of linseed oil mixed with two parts of paraffin, stirred together and brushed liberally on the wood.

Where there is risk of excessive drying out during construction, the timber should be coated with boiled linseed oil when erected, to prevent opening up. The timber built into a boat must be of good quality, properly seasoned and free from imperfections such as heartwood, sap, decay, insect attack, splits and shakes, which will affect its efficiency.

Woods commonly used for small boat construction in Britain, North America, Europe and Australasia are described in Appendix 2.

Plywood

Marine plywood is probably the most universally available timber for clinker planking small boats. It may have an almost uniform quality, free from blemishes, but its manufacture makes it relatively expensive.

Plywood is difficult to rebate successfully at the plank ends and needs careful sealing at the plank edges where the cores and gluelines are exposed. It cannot be steam bent, but slight compound curves are possible, the extent being determined by trial and depending on the thickness, number of laminates and the type of timber. Plywood must not be forced beyond creaking point, and it must be remembered that usually less than half the laminates are intended to resist side pressures and many of the inner cores are not of dense timber.

The bonding of marine plywood should be to British Standard Specification 1203 WBP, which means weather and boil proof, or to an equivalent standard. Test pieces are subjected to 72 hours' boiling before being allowed to cool and then the gluelines are knife-tested for quality of the bonds. British Standard Specification 1088 incorporates this boiling test and also specifies types of wood acceptable for face and core veneers used in making British plywood of marine quality. Typically, British-made marine plywood may have face veneers of makore, a closegrained, dense timber regarded as durable. Alternative face veneers may be khaya, sapele or utile. However, the standard permits core materials which may not be too durable, and the Dutch Bruynzeel plywood is considered by many to be excellent for boatbuilding as all the laminates are of durable timber.

Marine plywood is usually supplied in sheets 8 ft by 4 ft and thicknesses from 4 mm to 38 mm. Larger sheets can be obtained but are probably more expensive than the standard sizes, area for area. Plywood can be supplied scarphed and glued to make longer panels or it can be scarphed and glued on the bench to make up planks longer than panels. A thickness/scarph ratio of 1:12 is recommended, the work being done before the plank shape is marked out. British marine plywood should be marked near the edge with the maker's name and identification mark, the British Standard 1088 and the nominal thickness of the board. The current range is 4, 5. 6, 7, 8, 12, 15, 18, 20, 22, 25, 30, 38 mm.

Although all British-made plywood to BSS 1088 is bonded to withstand the WBP test, the surfaces and edges still need protection. Edges invariably expose some end-grain laminates and water is absorbed into these more readily than the edge-grain laminates. To prevent this the end grain must be filled with thinned glue, and when painting two additional undercoats should be applied to these edges. Plywood must be stored flat, clear of the floor, on battens in a dry and airy place.

Fastenings

The fastening of small boats requires careful attention and the old boatbuilders' saying 'Nail where you can, screw where you have to and bolt where you must' is sound advice.

Wood screws

In small boatbuilding, wood screws are principally used to fasten the garboard strakes to the centreline structure of hog and keel, sometimes alternating with clenched nails. They are also used to fasten the hog to the keel and the plank ends to the stem, transom and sternpost.

It is unwise to use brass screws for structural work to be immersed in salt water as these often lose their zinc content very quickly and the holding power of the screw threads diminishes. Bronze or hot-dipped galvanised steel wood screws should be used in all structural boat work. Bronze wood screws are readily available in all sizes likely to be needed in small boat building. Steel wood screws can sometimes still be obtained hot-dip galvanised, but if not it is best to buy steel screws and have them dipped at the nearest galvanising plant; usually these are accustomed to handling items ranging from very small to large. The cost is usually by weight with a minimum charge.

The electro-galvanised screws now commonly offered are not satisfactory for durable boatbuilding as the very thin zinc deposit is easily damaged when driving the screw.

Wood screws should always be driven into a hole bored to receive them and the hole in the member to be attached should be of a diameter to pass the shank of the screw. The hole in the member to which fastening is made should not be larger than the main body of the screw in way of its threads. The heads of wood screws, if countersunk, must be bored for the countersink in the face of the timber to bring the head just under flush to the wood surface. In small boats the screws in the plank ends at stem and transom are close to the ends of the planks and in hardening down the fastening the head must be well countersunk to avoid splitting the planking.

If galvanised screws are used the countersink should be deep enough to permit stopping over with a marine stopping or the traditional red and white lead putty. Wood screws should always be dipped in grease before driving and be driven to reasonable tightness but no more; the further half a turn may break the screw in the hole or distort the wood fibres between the threads, and the fastenings will lose effectiveness. A wood screw driven into end grain (with the direction of the grain) has less holding power than a nail.

The size of a wood screw fastening for boatwork has to be judged by the builder. It should have a hold on the member to which fastening is to be made of at least $1\frac{1}{2}$ times the thickness of the member being attached. For $\frac{1}{2}$ in. planking the screw should not be less than $1\frac{1}{4}$ in. long. As a guide to size, for a light dinghy hull to 12 ft length, no. 8 gauge wood screws are suitable for fastening the garboard strake and no. 6 gauge for plank end fastenings.

Bronze screws or other fastenings should not be used to attach steel or iron fittings such as rudder gudgeons, stem and keel bands under water as the electrolytic action between the metals when immersed in salt water will cause rapid action between the iron and the screw, and will eventually cause deterioration in adjacent timber.

Bolts

In small boat construction bolts are used to fasten the stem and apron together, the stem to the keel and hog, the deadwood (if any) to the keel and sternpost transom to sternpost, and in heavier work to fasten knees to thwarts and gunwale, breasthooks to gunwale, centreboard case sills and mast step to hog and keel.

Galvanised steel or iron bolts with countersunk, flat or hexagon heads, threaded at one end and tightened with a nut on a washer of the same material, are now commonly used. Bronze bolts are superior but are more costly. Brass or stainless steel bolts should not be used for structural fastenings. The remarks regarding galvanising and the use of brass as a structural fastening, quoted under screws, also apply.

Traditionally, many of the bolt fastenings in small boat construction were made from copper or iron rod driven through the parts to be joined, cut off with a margin at each end and riveted over copper or iron washers. This is now uncommon, but such fastenings were very durable, cheap and could be made without the use of a thread-cutting tool.

The galvanised steel, iron or bronze screw bolt is a better fastening. It can be set up easily and more tightly, and iron bolts will stand great strain and recover from it without harm. Both types of bolt are illustrated (9a, 9b), showing the method of counterboring for the head of a bolt and of the fitting of a dowel over it. The larger hole or counterbore should be drilled first with a centrebit, and the actual bolt hole next. If the bolt hole is drilled first the point of the bit will have nothing to grip and the centreline hole will be a ragged one. If the dowels are dipped in paint before driving they will last the life of the bolt. Bolts which are permanent in the construction should, after setting up, be lightly riveted over on the nuts and have a dab of paint brushed over them.

Bolts of lengths up to 6 in. can often be obtained from stock in diameters from $\frac{1}{4}$ in. to $\frac{1}{2}$ in; $\frac{5}{16}$ in. diameter is a common size for the centreline of dinghies.

Clenched (riveted) bolts of copper or bronze rod must fit tightly in the holes as they derive much of their holding power from this friction. Also, if a slack fit, they will bend in the hole and will not properly close the work. Such bolts should not be

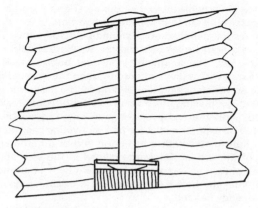

9a Clenched bolt

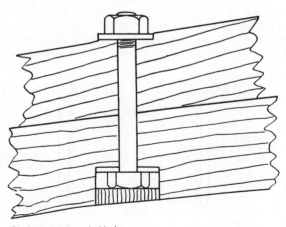

9b Nut and threaded bolt

too long in proportion to their diameter and a length of 20 times diameter is an average sensible proportion.

Holes for clenched bolts should be made with a twist drill to ensure a tight fitting bolt and the washers should be a tight fit on the rod. The length of individual bolts can be accurately measured with a piece of wire through the hole, adding about $\frac{3}{4}$ in. or so for clenching, depending on the diameter. The head is formed by placing the rod in a vice between two pieces of wood, with the rod projecting up about $\frac{3}{16}$ in. The washer is slipped on and a head is formed by riveting the rod down on to it by light blows with a ball-peen end of a hammer. The other end of the rod is afterwards placed in the vice and the sharp edges of the cut end are tapped down with a hammer to enable it to enter the hole easily. The bolt is of course driven from the end already headed.

Grommets made from caulking cotton twisted around the diameter of the bolt and coated with bedding paint or compound must be placed under the heads of bolts and under washers under nuts.

Nail fastenings

Nail fastenings may be of copper, galvanised iron or silicon bronze. British-made copper boat nails are of square section with a flat head, slightly countersunk underneath. European and Scandinavian boat nails are often of round section, with a similar head. A square or rectangular section nail is called a cut nail, a round section nail a wire nail; terms denoting methods of

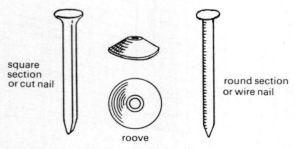

square section or cut nail

roove

round section or wire nail

10   Square and round section boat nails and a roove

manufacture (10). Cut nails are desirable because they have no tendency to turn in the hole when in position as fastenings, and their chisel points can be driven through hot bent timbers with less chance of splitting than from round wire nails.

Copper boat nails
Sizes often used in small boatbuilding
Square section with flat countersunk heads

Length (in.)	$\frac{5}{8}$	$\frac{3}{4}$	1	$1\frac{1}{8}$	$1\frac{1}{4}$	$1\frac{1}{2}$	$1\frac{3}{4}$	2	$2\frac{1}{4}$	$2\frac{1}{2}$
Gauge	16	16	14	13	13	13	12	11	11	10

Length (in.)	3	$3\frac{1}{2}$	4
Gauge	9	8	7

Range of stock sizes available

Length (in.)	$\frac{1}{2}$	$\frac{5}{8}$	$\frac{3}{4}$	$\frac{7}{8}$	$\frac{7}{8}$	1	1	1	1	$1\frac{1}{8}$	$1\frac{1}{8}$
Gauge	16	16	16	15	16	13	14	15	16	13	14

Length (in.)	$1\frac{1}{4}$	$1\frac{1}{4}$	$1\frac{1}{4}$	$1\frac{1}{4}$	$1\frac{1}{2}$	$1\frac{1}{2}$	$1\frac{1}{2}$	$1\frac{1}{2}$	$1\frac{1}{2}$	$1\frac{3}{4}$	$1\frac{3}{4}$	$1\frac{3}{4}$	$1\frac{3}{4}$
Gauge	12	13	14	15	11	12	13	14	15	11	12	13	14

Length (in.)	2	2	2	$2\frac{1}{4}$	$2\frac{1}{4}$	$2\frac{1}{4}$	$2\frac{1}{2}$	$2\frac{1}{2}$	$2\frac{1}{2}$	3	3	3	3	$3\frac{1}{8}$	$3\frac{1}{2}$
Gauge	10	11	12	10	11	12	10	11	12	9	10	11	12	8	9

Length (in.)	$3\frac{1}{2}$	4	4	4	5	6
Gauge	10	7	8	10	6	6

Copper boat nails are usually sold in 7 lbs bags up to $\frac{7}{8}$ in. length, and in 1 lb boxes above this size.

Copper rooves

Outside diameter of roove (in.)	$\frac{1}{4}$	$\frac{5}{16}$	$\frac{3}{8}$	$\frac{7}{16}$	$\frac{1}{2}$	$\frac{1}{2}$	$\frac{9}{16}$	$\frac{5}{8}$	$\frac{3}{4}$
For nail size	15	14	13	12	11, 10	9	8, 7	6	

Nail fastenings may be used in three ways:
1. As dead fastenings, i.e. driven completely through the member to be attached and part way through the member to which attachment is to be made. Dead nail fastenings are commonly used to attach the plank ends to the stem, apron and transom,

11 Square section nail ragged for improved holding

the garboard strake to the keel and hog, and the rubbing strakes to the gunwale. Galvanised nails hold well in these positions but are liable to rust stain the adjacent wood as the hammer blows of driving often break the coating of zinc. Silicon bronze ringed nails hold very well for this work and are of course most durable. If copper nails are driven as dead nails it is usual to 'rag' their shanks with an old chisel or knife to obtain a better hold with their smooth finish (11).

2. As turned nails. These should be of copper and are used to fasten planking to the bent frames, risings to bent frames, hull plank seams or lands, and sometimes knees and breasthooks to the thwarts, gunwales and transom. Turned nails are driven in holes bored through the member to be attached and, except in bent frames, through the member to which attachment is to be made. The nail head is driven close to the wood surface and a dolly is held against it while the point of the nail is turned over by hammer blows forming it into a staple shape (12). It is necessary that the point be turned twice as shown, as copper nails are soft and will tend to draw if clenched with a single turn. The nail must always be turned down with the direction of the grain, to enter it and lie almost flush. Turned nails must be exactly the right length to suit the thickness of wood being fastened and they must be cut nails, not wire nails.

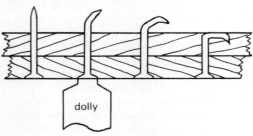

dolly

12   Turning a nail

24

3. As fastenings clenched on rooves or copper washers. These fastenings should be of copper as its elasticity and malleability make it easy to clench or rivet over. They are used to fasten the same items as turned nails and are fitted and driven in the same way except that the point of the nail has a copper roove driven over it and down its shank, the excess nail being cut off when the roove is firmly on the timber, when the end is clenched or riveted down onto the roove by hammer blows (13).

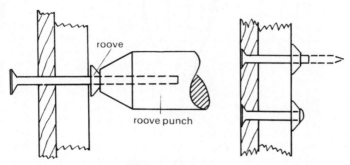

13   Driving and clenching a nail on a roove

Galvanised or bronze nails are not usually suitable for clenched or turned fastenings. Galvanised iron or steel is insufficiently malleable, though it is commonly used for plank fastenings in Norway and sometimes in America, due to cheapness and availability. Bronze nails are more malleable but usually made with a ribbed finish to the shank and are consequently likely to break if turned, besides being much more difficult to clench than a copper nail.

Rooved copper nail fastenings are best for the amateur, and after boring, the head of the nail should be driven flush with the wood surface. In hardwood the hole may need to be slightly countersunk. It is best for clenching to be done by two people, if possible; the clencher inside the boat and a helper or holder-on holding a dolly of substantial weight against the nailhead. A copper roove is placed in the point of the nail and is driven down it with a rooving iron or roove punch. (In American practice rooves are called burrs and a roove punch a burr set.)

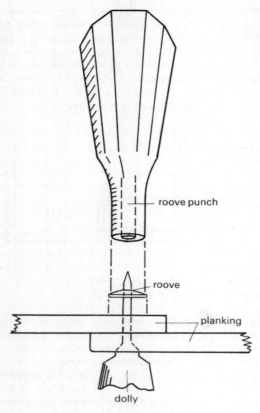

roove punch

roove

planking

dolly

14   Use of a roove punch and dolly

This grips the corners of a square nail and draws the head well
home to the wood surface (14). The roove must have a hole
small enough so that when it is driven over the point of the nail
and forced down firmly against the wood it will hold tightly until
the nail is headed and clenched.

The method of fitting rooves varies in some areas but the
only correct and efficient way is for the roove to be driven with

its apex towards the roove punch. After the roove is driven on, the tail of the nail is cut off with hand cutters, leaving about $\frac{3}{32}$ in. extending beyond the roove apex. The amount remaining must be just enough to form a good head and no more. If excess is left on it will tend to make the nail buckle in the wood. The tail is then riveted over with a succession of light taps of a small, well balanced hammer (about $\frac{1}{2}$ lb weight). Methods of clenching vary but an efficient sequence is to use the toe of the hammer to spread the tail out slightly over the roove and to finish with the ball-peen, rounding the clench neatly. The light taps are absorbed at the end of the nail and spread out evenly over the roove and the head thus formed draws the nail through the hole in the roove, drawing the members together by tightening the copper nail between its head and the roove, which compresses slightly within itself due to its conical shape and also depresses its edges slightly into the timber. During clenching the dolly is held firmly against the nail head with a steady pressure. Tightening of the fastening will be evident from the sound of the hammer blows changing to a sharper note. Heavy blows should not be given as they will flatten the roove and tend to compress the nail within its length, which will probably cause it to bend in the hole, and a slack fastening and a leak will result.

If too large a hammer is used and the blows are too heavy; if the nails are not clipped short enough or if the rooves are of incorrect size which will not hold firmly when forced down with the roove punch; the nails will buckle and cripple within the wood without drawing tight. In extreme cases this can split a plank land.

If the roove draws into the wood before the nail tightens a larger size of roove should be used. A few trials in clenching scrap pieces of planking together will confirm this and indicate the correct amount to be left when cutting off the tail of the nail.

Great care should be taken to avoid the hammer bruising the wood around the roove or the dolly slipping and bruising the outside surface of the planking.

Holding-up is tiring and helpers may become inattentive and hold on the wrong nail, resulting in the clencher driving the correct (and cut off) nail back and the roove falling off. This necessitates another nail being driven, but it can never be as tight in the hole as the first. Also, holders-on do not always see that the nail heads are settled flush with the surface of the wood.

Much small boatbuilding is carried out singlehanded, and it is best for various reasons to clench the nails in the plank seams as each strake is completed. This relieves the demoralising monotony of being faced with large numbers of nails to clench at once, and the plank seams will be tighter as, unless clenching is done as work progresses, there is risk of creeping in the seams and when the last seam is clenched distortion may be found.

Singlehanded, the nail is driven until the point is through the timber. The roove is put on with the rooving punch held against it and the nail is driven against the roove and punch, effectively driving the roove on in the same way as previously described. When the nail head is tight against the wood the punch is removed and the tail cut off. The combined punch and dolly is moved to be held against the head of the nail which is clenched as previously described. Before attempting to clench nails in a new boat those unfamiliar with clenching should practice on scrap timber lapped to simulate those in the boat and held in a bench vice.

The following sizes of copper nails are intended as a general guide for normal small boat building practice but may need to be varied to suit fine or heavier construction, or for widely varying qualities of timber.

For light hulls with up to $\frac{5}{16}$ in. thick planking—16 gauge nails. For average types of dinghies with $\frac{3}{8}$ in. thick planking—14 gauge nails for plank landings and 13 gauge nails for plank to bent frame fastenings. For hulls with $\frac{1}{2}$ in. thick planking—13 gauge nails. For long fastenings through knees, breasthooks and centreboard case sills—10–12 gauge nails.

Suitably sized twist drills may be used to bore holes for nail fastenings but many boatbuilders prefer to make their own drills from steel wire. If obtainable, square section steel wire $1\frac{1}{2}$ mm sided is suitable for 16 gauge to 13 gauge fastenings; cut off to a suitable length for the holes to be bored. If 16 gauge nails are to be used the wire should be filed off slightly at the corners; for larger gauges it should be left square.

The end must be filed to a chisel point of about 30 degrees, then hardened and tempered by being held in a flame until cherry red and plunged quickly in water. The oxidised film must then be cleaned from one side with emery cloth and the drill held close to the flame but not in it. The cleaned side will show a pale straw colour which quickly darkens. When this change of colour is reached the drill should be plunged into water. The change of colour from pale to dark occurs rapidly and it is best to plunge the drill as soon as the pale straw colour appears because by the time it is moved for quenching the colour will have darkened. It is only necessary to harden the first $\frac{3}{4}$ in. of the drill point. These wire drills will last and are generally self-clearing and easily sharpened when required.

Glues and adhesives

Glues to be used for boat construction and lamination of structural members should be of gap-filling resorcinol or phenolic types such as comply with British Standard Specification 1204 WBP (weather and boil proof), or other adhesive which has similar durability and can achieve a WBP bond. Resorcinal glues are capable of withstanding 72 hours boiling, have a dark glueline and are capable of filling a gap of approximately 1 mm without becoming brittle or cracking. Epoxy adhesives are now also widely used in boatbuilding.

Glues or adhesives must be mixed and applied in accordance with the manufacturer's instructions and with regard to the prevailing temperature and hardening requirements. Attention must be given to the application techniques for the species of timber being glued and the manufacturer's advice should be sought in the bonding of different timbers and the effect of preservatives on their materials.

The timber to be bonded must be clean and dry with the jointing surfaces properly prepared and free from dust and grease. The adhesive must be evenly applied and the joint closed within the manufacturer's recommended closing time to obtain a thin and uniform glueline. Sufficient cramps or other pressure devices must be used and the pressure must not be relieved until the joint is set. Superfluous adhesive must be wiped from the work with a dry cloth. If allowed to adhere and harden it will inhibit the paint or varnish coatings, when these are applied. With any adhesives, some experiment should be made before using them in construction. Plain bonds and scarphs should be made in scrap wood and afterwards tested for strength.

A widely used boatbuilding adhesive in America is General Mills Versamid 140 or 125, and an epoxy resin of medium high or high viscosity, such as Union Carbide's Bakelite epoxy ERL-2774, 11000-14000 cps at 77° F. A high viscosity or thick mix will not drain out of vertical joints. A mix of 40 parts Versamid to 60 parts epoxy resin is considered desirable, though these proportions are not too critical. This is slow in setting, usually overnight at room temperatures, but faster in summer temperatures. 125 Versamid is of higher viscosity than 140 and acts faster as a hardener. The Versamids are non-irritating to human skin.

A remarkable epoxy adhesive named Chem-Tec T.88 has been formulated for boatbuilding by G Schindler, 4481 Greenwold Road, Cleveland, Ohio 44121 (a chemist who is also an amateur boatbuilder). It is a modified epoxy-polyamid material with claimed ability to cure at very low temperatures. Simple 1:1 mixing, chemical inertness, insensitivity to water immersion and immunity to microrganisms are also claimed besides being non-corrosive and non-irritating to human skin. Chem-Tec T. 88 can be applied to moist timber and will even cure under water. Wood steamed for bending does not need drying for several days before use. When applied to damp wood the adhesive must be thoroughly worked into the surface. It will cure at temperatures as low as 30° F without loss of strength. At 70°F it hardens in 6—8 hours and achieves full strength in 24 hours. Pot life at this temperature is about 45 minutes, yet a joint may be cramped more tightly for 2 hours after adhesive application. Joint thickness is not critical and there is no danger of starved joints from tight clamping, yet open joints with the adhesive thickened to a paste consistency cure without reduction in strength.

30

Laminated members

The layers comprising a lamination should be of the same type of timber with approximately equal moisture content of about 15 per cent. The grain of the layers must be parallel to the length of the member. In laminations for small craft the layers should be continuous, but if any joining is necessary the layers should be scarphed. When the layers are bent to produce members of curved shape the thickness of each layer must be such that it will not be overstressed in forming and a satisfactory interlaminar bond will be achieved. The following are recommended layer thicknesses and radii for laminated members:

Radius of curvature (in.)	Thickness of layers (in.)
17	$\frac{3}{16}$
23	$\frac{1}{4}$
38	$\frac{3}{8}$
54	$\frac{1}{2}$
90	$\frac{3}{4}$
125	1

The best method of laminating a stem for a small boat is to lay out the profile shape full size on a piece of scrap plywood about $\frac{1}{2}$ in. thick. A parallel line about $\frac{1}{2}$ in. outside the face of the stem is also marked and the wood backing blocks for cramping against are fitted up to this line, being screwed through the plywood from underneath. Blocks cut from 2 in. by 4 in. timber are suitable, fastened with $2\frac{1}{2}$ in. no. 12 or 14 gauge wood screws. They must be firmly screwed to resist cramping pressures, particularly if a resorcinol glue is used. The blocks should be fixed on the outside of the profile so that the cramps draw the laminates into a cavity. A form batten is fixed around the faces of the blocks and well waxed to prevent the adhesive from sticking to it. The plywood base should also be well waxed. After preliminary cramping the laminates are tapped down with a wood block and hammer to rest snugly against the plywood base. The adhesive should be applied liberally as it is easier to clean off glue but difficult to use a glue-starved member.

Laminated knees are strong and look well if carefully made. A form must be made for bending and gluing the layers, which should be about $\frac{1}{8}$ in. thick for a small boat's knee. These build up a block from which the finished knee is cut. The form is in two parts, representing the outside and inside shape. These are cramped towards each other with the laminates assembled between. The forms must be well waxed before applying the adhesive or it will stick. Canadian rock elm, spruce, oak or mahogany are suitable woods from which laminated knees may be made.

2 Plans and Laying Off

A builder may also design the boat to be built but it is more probable that he will build from plans supplied from a designer. The author is willing to assist builders who have difficulty in obtaining plans for constructing clinker boats.

Plans for building any boat should be as detailed as possible and for small craft up to about 20 ft length it is useful if the lines are drawn to a scale of $1\frac{1}{2}$ in. to 1 ft as this ensures accurate fairing. Many professional boatbuilders prefer plans drawn to this scale as it means that $\frac{1}{8}$ in. on scale is equal to 1 actual in., and with a woodwork rule divided into $\frac{1}{32}$ in. they can scale a drawing to within $\frac{1}{4}$ in. However, prints of original drawings should *never* be scaled as the paper distorts in printing and only the written dimensions are true. If the boat is built from a design, the designer will have prepared a table of offsets from which the lines can be accurately set out.

The usual plans supplied for a small boat design are:

The lines plan. Showing profile, half-breadth and sections through the hull and giving all dimensions and detail to lay off the lines full size.

Table of offsets. Carefully measured dimensions for the sheer, keel, waterlines, buttock lines, bow lines and diagonal lines, measured about the baseline and centreline.

Hull construction plan. Full details of the structure in profile, plan and at least one section, besides details of intricate parts, i.e. deadwood, stem sections, centreboard case, etc.

Mast and spar construction. All dimensions and sections through any spars which are not round in section or are built hollow.

Ironwork and fittings plan (or plans). Full details of all items such as centreplate, mainsheet horse, gooseneck, centreboard pin, tiller clasp, rudder pintles and gudgeons, etc.

Sail plan. Indicating complete details. Profile of sails on the mast and spars, fully dimensioned. A useful plan from which to judge the finished appearance of a boat.

Rigging plan. Details of all standing and running rigging; sizes and materials.

Laying off or lofting

If the lines of a boat are 'laid down', which means drawn full size and faired, as they should be before commencing to build, any error in the designer's offsets is found and corrected. Some slight adjustments in the offsets are to be expected as these have been measured from a plan probably drawn to scale and the width of a fine pencil line magnified 12 or 16 times becomes appreciable, so accuracy of lofting is essential. Variations of $\frac{1}{8}$ in. actual measurement may be revealed but will resolve themselves in adjustment during fairing.

One of the principal functions of laying off is preparation for making the moulds which are an important part of clinker boatbuilding. These are transverse sections, accurately made in wood to the boat's shape at intervals along its length, to which the planking is made to conform as closely as possible. Many builders will avoid as much loft work as possible but it is at least necessary to set out the transverse sections at the building mould positions from the table of offsets.

Moulds will not need to be built for every transverse station on the drawings, where they are needed for fairing the lines. The number of moulds required will depend on the size and shape of the hull but an amateur will need an adequate number, usually three besides the transom in a 10–14 ft boat and four in a boat 14–20 ft, with the possibility that if the larger boat has much shape at the bow, and perhaps at the stern, an extra mould will be wanted, probably on a half-station.

Professional boatbuilders of the past often built open boats up to 20 ft by using only a half midship mould which was held in place to check the form as work progressed. Although these men developed great skill and a wonderful eye for shape, these hulls are not so true to shape as one built over a number of moulds and the principal reason for this extreme simplicity was cost, as laying off was not required and it gave uninterrupted

34

space for the man to work without fixed moulds getting in his way. The difference between this traditional boatbuilder and the painstaking amateur is that while the traditionalist was producing a form of boat of which his experience had taught him to have a clear conception, the amateur is usually building from someone else's design.

Whenever there is doubt on the number of moulds to be made it is always desirable to include those next to the stem and stern, particularly in full-bodied boats. These end moulds greatly assist the preservation of accurate shape at the end planking. The distance apart of the other moulds should be generally about 3 ft.

The following parts will also need to be drawn or 'laid down' full size.

Stem

This will usually be as shown in (15). All waterlines must be shown and additional waterlines drawn, if required, near the round of the forefoot, where additional vertical stations will also be needed. These additional waterlines and stations can be lightly pencilled in on the lines plan as thought necessary, and the dimensions picked off and laid down full size.

The line x-x is the datum or baseline from which height measurements are taken. In small boats this is usually taken as the lowest point of the underside of keel and it also corresponds to the upper face of the building stocks. The full size laying off of the stem should show all details of the stem construction as this information will be used when the stem is worked and set up. At the same time a full size plan view of the forward end waterlines and half breadth must be laid down (16). This will later be necessary for obtaining the bevels for the stem and the stem plank rebate, apron and stem knee, if these are fitted.

Body plan

Designers usually draw the transverse sections of a boat's lines on each side of a common centreline. However, the boatbuilder may prefer to lay them down as shown in (17) as the sections through the keel and hog, and the rebate sections, are laid out on this drawing and this arrangement of sections keeps

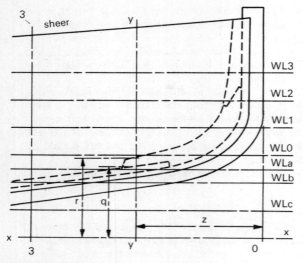

15 Profile of laying off stem

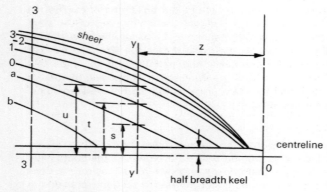

16 Plan view of laying off stem

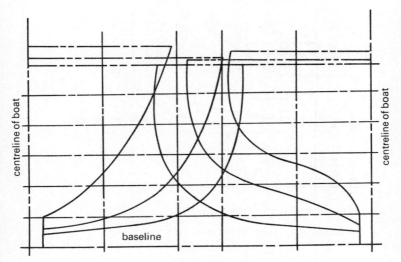

17 Preferred method of laying off hull sections

the centreline details apart and provides two margins on which heights and thicknesses may be noted. In all sections the half breadth of keel is drawn and the body sections always fair to and stop at these half breadths *and not at the centreline*. In designs where the keel moulding or thickness varies, as in many sailing dinghies, care is necessary to ensure accuracy, as a mistake in this region might cause a mould to be set too high or low and result in much trouble and discouragement later. To emphasise this (18) is an enlarged lower part of (19). Section 3 is assumed to be lightly drawn and all crossings with the waterlines and diagonals are assumed to be correct. The distance is checked from the baseline with the same height as shown on the profile at full size and the half breadth of keel is lifted from the half breadth on the station. From the profile the height of the keel at that point is noted and marked down and the height is also noted on the side of the scrieve board for reference when setting up the keel on the stocks. The siding of the keel and the hog are also marked on the body plan.

37

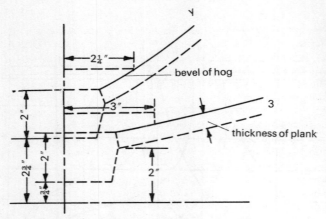

18 Sections through stem, enlarged from (17)

19 Sections through forward end of boat in way of stem

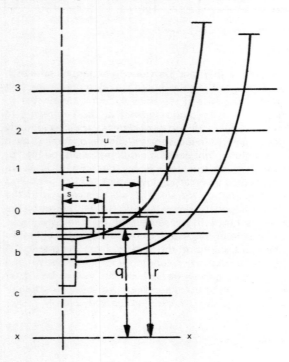

The shape of the hull which is drawn is the line to the outside of planking and the thickness of the plank must be set out inside this line. This is done at a number of spots and a batten put round for marking it. By this means the full details of the shape of keel and hog are obtained full size for each station, including the bevel of the hog for the garboard strake. These bevels can be lifted with a bevel and transferred to a piece of wooden board for use and reference when working the hog to shape. The section also now gives the shape of the mould from the hog to the sheer. When all the mould stations have been marked out the moulds can be made, but before cutting the timber it is best to check the sheerline finally by measuring its half breadth at each station and its height above the baseline. The moulds should be carried about 1 in. above the sheerline, but the point of the sheerline must be accurately marked to finish the planking in the fair curve which was drafted on the lines plan. Sheerlines are difficult to visualise in a three-dimensional drawing and it is possible that adjustment may be required when the boat is planked, but sheering down should only be done after considerable consideration of the appearance of the sheer from all angles.

The full sized laying off is conveniently done on one or two sheets of 8 ft by 4 ft plywood or hardboard with a moderately hard pencil. Alternatively, if space is restricted, it can be done on sheets of heavy paper stuck together, but a rigid floor is preferable. Tools required for laying off include a 2 ft rule marked in inches down to $\frac{1}{16}$ in. A wood or metal straightedge of about 6 ft minimum length, a try square to get the station lines square to the base and centreline (this may be made by setting out a triangle with sides of $3 \times 4 \times 5$ units, making a right angle), a batten about 4 ft long and about $\frac{3}{4}$ in. by $\frac{3}{16}$ in. section. A section and another about as long as the boat if possible but at least $\frac{2}{3}$ the length and of approximately $\frac{3}{4}$ in. by $\frac{1}{4}$ in. section. A dozen 5–6 in. wire nails with sharpened points will make excellent batten pins for driving gently into plywood to hold the battens; alternatively weights may be used. The parallel lines of the waterlines and buttocks must be accurate and it is best to draw these in hard pencil or ink as there will be some rubbing out during laying off. Traditionally, laying off was done with fine lines drawn with well sharpened, white paint chalk on a black painted floor, but the method described above is best for amateur builders.

Drawings should be made of the outlines of the breasthook, quarter knees, thwart knees, stem, apron, and stern knee and stiff paper templates made of their shapes. As all grown timber tends to warp after sawing, these templates should be cut well outside the pencil lines to allow a margin for distortion. Each template must be marked with the thickness or siding of the member and the number of pieces to be cut to that template. These must be taken to a timber yard which has oak or hackmatack crooks, or turns, and probably it will be necessary for the boatbuilder to try them against whatever stock is available as few crooks are saved nowadays when most top and lop, or branch timber, is burned when a tree is felled, or is sold to firewood merchants for cutting up as logs. Assuming some suitable crooks have been found, the shapes are cut out on a bandsaw and the members stood on their sides to dry out and season until wanted. The grain of these naturally grown crooks must follow the shape of the templates as closely as possible.

The siding (or width) of the stem and apron, stem knee or after deadwood may not be specified on the plans as their shape is governed by the lines endings and the sidings are obtained from the laid off lines. For example, the stem knee siding at the keel (15) is obtained by measuring on the full size profile its distance from station O and transferring this to the full size half breadth drawing, striking a line across as illustrated. The half breadth will be on that line and as the height of the keel on the profile is between levels a and O, it is obvious the width lies between these two waterlines on the full size body plan. The hull section at point y can then be drawn.

This procedure is detailed separately (19) to avoid confusion but is of course shown with the same framework of waterlines, and centreline and stations. As previously explained it is obtained by setting off on each waterline its breadth at the section (s, t, u) and the heights of keel and sheerline from the profile. Joining these points results in the hull section at y and at the required thickness inside this the planking thickness is set out. The heights of the top and bottom of the heel of the knee (r, q) are measured and, marking the line across for each, the width or siding at this point is obtained. By marking out on this section the heights of keel and hog, their sections at that point can also be obtained.

A similar use of the three views (profile, plan and section) of a boat's lines enables any dimension at any place to be obtained. Although usually the work is shaped from dimensions taken at the stations already shown by the designer, it is easy to draw a special section at any other point which is not a station, to get required information. The amateur builder must become familiar with this and may be helped by comparing on the profile, half breadth and body section views the corresponding dimensions marked with similar characters. All the views are interdependent and each provides two dimensions, thus:

Length (forward and aft) on profile plan and half breadth plan.
Breadth on body plan and half breadth plan.
Height on body plan and profile plan.

Once this simple principle is understood there will be no difficulty in setting out from the lines the desired part, without rules or explanations. Laying off is the foundation from which a well shaped, accurately built boat is constructed and is worth careful study. There are some boatbuilders, both amateur and professional, who can read lines in a general way but become confused when it is necessary to develop details from them.

Moulds

Moulds are best made of well seasoned, dry, soft pine. Wide old house floorboards, shelves or even packing case timber would make good moulds. Plywood is not recommended, except for straps, as although it will move very little, it is not easy to bevel accurately, does not accept nail fastenings readily and its surface is not easy to mark when transferring the section shape from the floor.

For small boats pine $\frac{1}{2}$ in. to $\frac{5}{8}$ in. thick is adequate. Although moulds do not need to be heavy they should be stiff, as they are subject to much strain at times: $2\frac{1}{2}$ in. by $\frac{3}{4}$ in. makes a rigid top

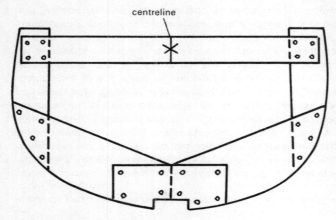

20 Method of making a transverse mould

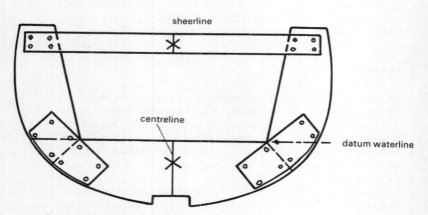

21 Improved method of making a transverse mould

spall for a mould up to 4 ft 6 in. beam. The lower piece will notch over the hog and must be neatly sawn and chiselled out to the correct height. If too much is accidentally cut away a wood chock must be fastened across at the correct level.

Methods of constructing moulds are shown in (20) and (21); (21) is best as there is no joint in the width of the bottom piece, and as it has one plane face, no bevelling of the edges is required. As the waterlines and half breadth in plan view are curves, a mould with a plane face can always be positioned on the side of the mould station towards amidships, with its face on the station line (22). But if the mould face has two levels (as in 20) either one or other of the pieces will have to be bevelled if it is to present the curve in correct position on the station line. This mould is sometimes made with butt joints and straps at the sides as well as at the bottom, but so many pieces make it difficult to assemble accurately compared with (21).

It is convenient to make moulds so that the planed upper

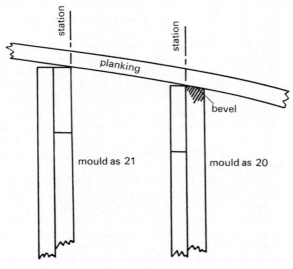

22　Comparison of mould faces (20, 21)

edge of the lower piece always corresponds with a datum waterline and the planed top edge of the upper cross piece corresponds with the sheerline. Then, a straightedge laid along the bottom pieces of the moulds should touch them all and, if so, they are all at the correct level relative to each other. If a strong batten straightedge is made the moulds can be fastened to it, which will aid setting up.

A long spirit level on the batten will show if they are longitudinally level on the stocks and the spirit level can also be placed transversely on the top of the lower piece to see that the moulds are level transversely. These are advantages when setting up as everything is rather loose and each alteration seems to bring need for more. This method is much preferred to setting up the tops of the lower spalls to a stretched line.

When the pieces of the mould are prepared, butted together, strapped and fastened with steel screws, the shape of the mould section has to be transferred to it accurately from the full size section laid off on the floor. The easiest method is to draw a centreline on the lower piece of the mould, squaring it across the edge of the wood. Copper or steel tacks are laid with heads around the line of the full size section on the floor, and the rough mould carefully placed over them with its centreline corresponding with that on the floor. The builder gently presses and hammers on the back of the mould making the tack heads bite into the soft pine. When lifted off the tacks will be adhering to the mould and will have made marks in it. A batten is bent round the marks, a line pencilled in and the mould sawn out just clear of the line before finishing off with a fine set smoothing plane in a vice. This may seem a crude method but it is very accurate and was used in shipyards for intricate moulds before the days of optical marking.

The moulds can also be made in segments which are strapped together after they are marked and cut, assembly being carried out on the full size section on the floor, the straps being tack-nailed together before final fastening with screws. With either method the mould shape must be carefully checked against the full size laid off section on the floor.

If the boat is to be built bottom up, the moulds must be carried straight from the sheerline to a datum or baseline which is marked on the sheer profile, parallel to the stocks at a convenient height above them, and the height to this is measured from the body plan at each mould. When removed and set up on the stocks they will have the waterlines level and be correctly positioned.

3   The Centreline Structure

Boatbuilding proper commences with working the centreline, and here it should be remembered that the commonest faults in amateurs are their impatience and neglect to completely finish (with certain necessary exceptions which will be mentioned) each part as building proceeds. No piece should be fastened until it is properly finished and cleaned off. Work which is simple to do at a bench becomes difficult and sometimes impossible when the item is fixed in place, resulting in ugly omissions. Working with the aim of leaving as little as possible to the final finishing will help to maintain a high standard of finish, besides saving much tedious work at the end of the job.

The amateur has the advantage over the professional in that his time costs nothing so he can afford to lavish it on his creation and make a thoroughly good job. He will probably make mistakes but should not be reluctant to discard members which he spoils or which are defective, replacing them with correctly made items.

Stem

In small boats the stem usually has curve in some part of its profile and traditionally, if possible, should be cut from a grown crook with grain approximating to the final shape. Alternatively it may be laminated from, say, $\frac{1}{4}$ in. or $\frac{3}{8}$ in. thick pieces of continuous length from the stemhead to the keel scarph, and possibly of sufficient width to incorporate the apron and stem knee (or deadwood) in one member. A stem should be made of a suitable hardwood as, apart from prolonging the longitudinal strength of the keel, it connects the forward sides of the boat and must also take inevitable chafe and abuse throughout the boat's life.

Depending on the size and availability of suitable timber, the grown stem is often made from three pieces: the stem proper, the stem knee or fore deadwood, and the apron piece (23). The stem knee backs up the joint between keel and stem, to 'succour it', as old boatbuilders said, and is usually cut from timber with suitable grain shape or is laminated separately, though this is unusual.

The apron piece is the continuation of the stem knee, strengthening the stem and provides a landing for the side planking ends which are at a wider angle than the bottom planking. If the stem and apron were combined in one piece of timber this would be difficult to work, and perhaps to obtain. As

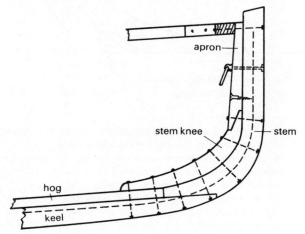

23 Typical stem construction

an apron is usually almost straight it can be worked from straight-grained timber. English elm was often used in British working boats. Oak, mahogany or iroko are also commonly used for aprons.

In much traditional work, the stem was just fitted on the top of the keel and fastened to it by two heavy gauge nails or screws through the toe and by a wooden treenail (or pin) or screws through the spur left on the forward edge of the lower stem to cover the end of the keel (24). If a suitable crook was not available the stem might be sawn from the butt of a tree, wide enough to provide the sweep of forefoot desired. Although

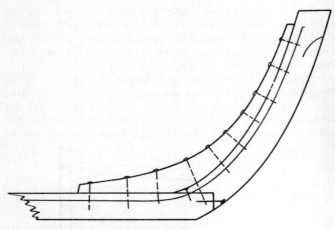

24   Traditional stem construction

this would be short-grained it was considered efficient if backed by the stem knee. However, this is not recommended practice.

Before the stem proper was finally set up it was common practice to beard off the sides, from the face nosing width back to the inner face width, except where left square at the stemhead. A gauge line was marked from the inner face on both sides of the stem as a guide for the plank rebate line. At the lower part of the stem the line would be modified to fair into the keel rebate, or perhaps might cut across the stem knee. The stem knee and apron were then fastened to the stem and the assembly set on the keel where the centrelines of each member must coincide and the stem be checked vertically with a plumbob. The plank rebate was cut out to suit as the hull planking progressed—an unsophisticated method suited to skilled men in a hurry but unsuitable for amateur boatbuilders.

The stem assembly and the forward end of the keel and hog is the most difficult part of building a small wooden boat, but the amateur builder can approach it confidently providing he is willing to methodically and carefully set out the various members, always checking everything at least once before cutting. The rebate and the rebate bevels for the planking is usually the

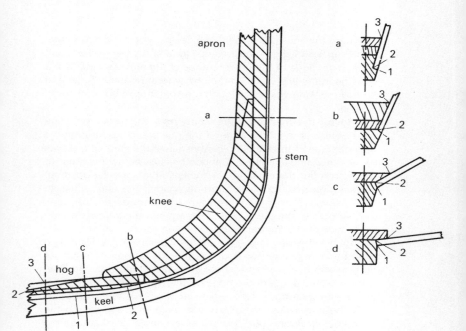

25 Stem rebate arrangements

most difficult to understand and dictates the arrangement, sizes and sectional shapes of the stem assembly, so must be considered first.

The illustration (25) clarifies the change of bevels of the rebate from amidships, where the plank fits in the rebate formed by the keel and hog, to the stem where it is almost vertical. The constructional arrangement of the faying surface of plank in the rebate amidships and at the upper part of the stem will be readily understood, but the varying bevels of the rebate throughout the radius of the stem and in the rockered forepart of the keel needs careful study. The area on which the planking bears (the faying surface) is shaded (25) and shows that, on this boat, the hull planking bears against the hog, stem and apron; though this will vary depending on the construction of the forward end of different boats. The lines marked No. 1, 2 and 3 aid in tracing the change. No. 1, the rebate line, is always

49

shown on the lines plan profile of a design and is the outer edge of the surface of the hull planking. No. 2 is the back rebate and is the upper edge of the inner surface of the hull planking. No. 3 is the bearding line which is the line where the inner surface of the hull planking ceases to touch the keel, hog, stem and apron (if fitted).

To follow the changes of the rebate trace the back rebate line No. 2, which is the inner edge of the hull planking. At station a the inner face of the planking bears against the stem and leaves it at the bearding line No. 3. Section b is just below the stem to keel scarph but the back rebate line is still in a similar position. However, part of the plank is fitting against the hog, which in this position is scarphed between the apron and the keel. Another part of the plank is bearing against the apron. Section c is in way of the keel and hog only, and the cut rebate is very shallow but the lowering angle of the hull planking is allowing a wider bearing against the hog. Section d is further aft in way of the keel and hog, and the rebate need not be cut into the keel as the lowered angle of the hog and the vertical side of the keel form a wide bearing surface and a suitable close-fitting rebate.

All the way round the plank has a bearing surface on the centreline structure but the bevel or angle of this bearing surface is altering at each waterline and section through the stem and keel. The width or siding of the stem or apron at its inside face should be much greater than the width of the stem at the rebate line (25). In some boats parallel stems are fitted, rebated for the planking, and often a narrow, angular space results between the inside of the planking and the stem, particularly at the round of forefoot. This harbours dirt, is difficult to clean and paint and can induce rot. If the apron or combined stem and apron cannot be obtained in sufficient width, an alternative is to fit cheek pieces or filling pieces, glued and screwed to the sides of the stem to increase the bearing surface for planking (26).

The stem is set out for shaping by drawing true sections at desirable intervals, usually at the waterlines and stations, and joining these with lines to indicate where it is to be cut. The selected crook, or alternatively lamination, is prepared for marking by having the forward face and sides squared and smoothed. A full size, thick paper pattern drawing of the stem

50

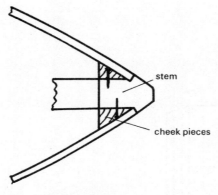

26   Stem cheek pieces

profile is made and laid over it, adjusted and tacked down firmly so that the forward edge of the stem can be marked on it with a fine bradawl; also the waterlines, the rebate line and the outline of the stem scarph. Remove the pattern and pencil in the lines, squaring the waterlines across the stem face and across the back, joining them across the opposite side of the stem, where they must exactly correspond. The rebate line must also be transferred on to the opposite side, where it crosses the waterlines. It is best to accurately measure these dimensions for transfer by marking on a piece of stiff card or paper, or with screw dividers, rather than with a rule.

If the paper template of the stem profile is carefully made it can be reversed and the lines pricked through on the opposite face of the stem, but care must be taken to ensure that the two sets of markings are exactly level by squaring the waterlines accurately across the stem faces.

The centreline of the boat is carried down the face of the stem and the half breadths of the stem's forward face are drawn in (27). These widths will probably broaden towards the scarph, where the keel width (siding) is approached.

In many traditional working boats the stemhead for about $\frac{1}{6}$ of the stem height below the sheer was left square and shaped off below it (24). This is unusual in a pleasure boat unless a

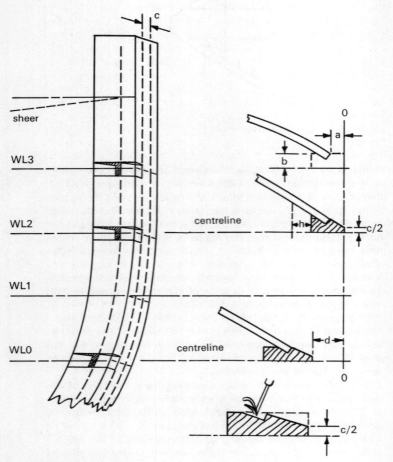

27 Setting out the stem

bowsprit is fitted, when it is useful for bolting the gammon iron through the stemhead.

The bearding line must be marked at each waterline (27). This should be set out full size. From a line representing the centreline of the half breadth plan set off a parallel line equal to the half siding of the stem (b in the drawing). Draw a line to represent station O or the forward side of the stem and from this mark a spot at the distance a, where the rebate line touches the stem at this particular waterline or, conversely, where the waterline cuts the stem. A bevel or a stiff jointed rule (an engineer's steel rule is useful) is set to the angle of the last few inches of the waterline where it cuts the stem, using the centreline as the base for the other arm of the bevel or rule. Transfer the angle obtained to the detail sketch at a and draw parallel to it the thickness of planking, which line will also cut the stem. Square off the end of the planking and join the rebate line to a spot set off at the forward side of the stem to indicate the half breadth of the stem's forward face. This gives a section of the stem at this waterline. Where the inner face of the planking leaves the siding of the stem is the bearding line—an old term illustrating the point from which the stem was 'bearded off'. Transfer these dimensions measured from the station line to the stem and also the opposite waterline. Do the same for all other waterlines and obtain a series of spots for the bearding line.

If there is an apron or stem knee behind the stem the thickness of this can also be set out at the various waterlines, as at h, and the line drawn transversely to cut the inside of planking to obtain the half siding which will be needed later. Besides reinforcing the stem, the knee enables greater width or siding to be given at the heel of the stem without cutting and working with exaggerated siding at the heel; difficult to work in one piece and more difficult to obtain in natural grown form.

It will be noted that although the lower face of the turn of the stem recedes from station O, this is still used as the datum from which measurements are made for setting out the stem. The setting out can be done on the full size, laid off, half breadth drawing, but as the waterlines are close together at the stem it will result in confusion of lines and probably mistakes. It will almost certainly be necessary to obtain a vertical section through the heel of the stem, depending on its shape; and this should be done as in (18). The spots representing the bearding line are joined by bending a thin batten through them and pencilling in the line. The stem scarph should now be cut as this is best done while the crook is still square sided. The saw should be entered in one side to make a vertical guide for the saw while it cuts through from the opposite face. When sawn it must be tested with a square and pared until it is vertical when set up on the keel. Some adjustment may afterwards be necessary, but accuracy must be used in cutting the scarph.

To cut the stem rebate a small piece of wood is prepared of the same thickness as the finished planking, about 6 in. by 1 in. wide, with its ends accurately squared. The stem is cramped to the bench and cutting commences at each waterline in turn (27). The chisel should be reversed at each cut to work out a vee, cutting back until the rebate line on one side and the bearding line on the other is reached. The work must be checked frequently with the plank template as a gauge. The rebate has a small steep face which must be at right angles to the long, shallow face which runs out at the bearding line. The builder must guard against the tendency to cut the steep side too vertical, particularly around the turn of the forefoot. When the template just fits in, cut away the slope from the rebate line to the finished breadth of the forward edge of the stem. It is best to saw down near the marks with a tenon saw, allowing the bulk of the wood, between waterlines, to be cut away carefully and cleaned off with chisel and plane.

When the rebates at all the waterlines have been cut as described, the intervening timber is planed or sawn away until all faces are fair. Use of a tenon saw will save much chiselling time, and a short rebate plane is useful for cleaning out the straighter parts. The thickness of line should always be left showing after cutting. The face of the stem will be planed to a finish after the boat is planked. Slight excess material in the rebate will be pared away as the planks are fitted, but if the bevels have been accurately obtained there is need for very little excess.

It is easy to work a stem on the bench but when it is set up, chiseling it becomes very difficult. The stem above the sheerline should not be bevelled off or, of course, rebated. It is best left

54

square until the boat is finished. In some designs the stem siding decreases from the sheer to the keel. This would be set out on the waterlines on the half breadth plan and care must be taken to obtain an adequate landing of plank in the rebate; 1 in. is a minimum on the stem itself, even if it is backed by an apron or stern knee to give additional landing.

There remains on the stem the material at the after side of the bearding line. If the design has an apron or stem knee, this will have to be cut away to this line to permit them to fay up to it. If the material were left on and the apron or knee were fayed up and fitted to the inside of planking on each side, there would be a sealed space on each side which would rapidly cause rot and decay. If an apron or knee is not fitted and the material is left on for strength, sliver or cheek pieces must be glued and fastened to the sides of the stem (26). The widths are marked at waterlines and then they are pared away to the correct bevels to support the planking. It is best to fasten these with screws rather than nails, besides glue, for if the screws are not sunk deeply enough below the surface of the rebate they can be removed, to be bored deeper and sunk safely out of the way of chisels.

Before sawing off the back of the stem the LWL mark should be transferred across the sides of the stem (as this will have been chiseled away in shaping the stem) to join the mark remaining on the forward face of the stem. This will be needed when setting up.

The curve of the forefoot should be finished to the correct profile if found necessary. Before leaving the stem, measure and mark off on the heel the centres for any bolts. If the stem scarph is covered by a knee this will not be required.

If an apron or stem knee are fitted these can now be shaped. The after profile is pricked through from a template drawing, but the forward profile can be scribed from the after side of the stem which is laid on the timber. The LWL must be set out on the apron to give a registration mark for fitting apron and stem accurately together, and should be squared across its after face so it can be seen when the side marks have been cut away in shaping. When cut in profile the apron or knee will need paring and rasping to get a good faying surface to the stem. To ensure it going back in the same place during fitting it is best to drill

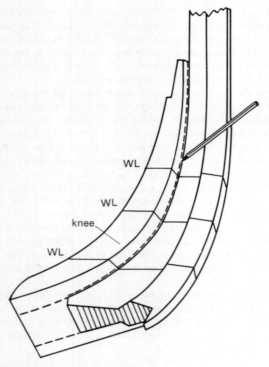

WL

WL

knee

WL

28   Scribing stem knee from the stem

and fasten the apron or knee to the stem by two temporary
screws. To assist in finally checking, the after face of the stem
may be chalked and the apron or knee pressed hard onto it.
When taken apart the high spots will show on the knee and can
be pared away. When the parts are fitted the apron or knee is
scribed from the stem (28) to get the forward line for bevelling
the sides. The widths of the after faces will be obtained as
described for setting out the stem rebates (27h). The breadths
or sidings of the keel are obtained as in (18, 19), but in this case
it is best not to cut right back to the breadths, but to leave a

small margin to be planed off when set up and checked with a batten. There is possibility of error because the enlarged ends of the waterline curves have been taken as straight lines at certain angles, but any curve the planks may have at this point is very slight. At the knee, the surface is well aft of the point at the stem where the angle was taken and the angle of the curve is constantly changing. There is little slope to the curve of the body at the vertical section and its distance from the centre alters rapidly for a small variation in height, so a small margin is allowed for later adjustment.

If an apron is fitted it should be scarphed to the stem knee. Often a plain bevel scarph is made (29c). The apron is carried up to the sheerline and the breasthook butts against it. A throat bolt or clench fastening is fitted through the breasthook, apron and stem.

In some traditional American small clinker-built craft such as the New England wherry, the stem was often made in two vertical pieces. The plank ends fitted to the inner or true stem and the outer false stem was fitted afterwards and fastened through the inner stem. This method was rarely if ever used in traditional British practice but eases the difficulty of cutting rebates, and with modern adhesives and care can be as efficient as conventional construction.

Scarph of stem to keel

The type and arrangements of scarphs should be indicated on the plans, but if this is left to the builder's choice the following may be considered, remembering that scarphs should be as simple as possible.

(29a) A traditional method now seldom used, where the stem and keel are halved together. Stronger than a horizontal scarph of similar length as the heel is locked and the bolts are only in shear. In a horizontal scarph a direct blow will put the bolts in tension and if of copper they will probably distort permanently.

(29b, c) Common traditional arrangements with a horizontal scarph, without a stem knee. (29c) has an apron fitted.

(29d, g) Typical arrangements where the scarph is backed by a stem knee or deadwood.

(29e) Methods occasionally used to avoid having a wide heel to the knee for craft with very full bow sections and a deep forefoot. The stem knee is set on a shallow but wide solepiece which provides a bearing surface for the planking and dispenses with the fitting of cheek pieces. This is used where a boat is of such shape that a stem knee cannot be obtained with sufficient width, but as knees of any desired width can be laminated it is now seldom used.

(29f) Stopwater; a softwood dowel driven tight in a hole through the scarph in way of the rebate line. The hole is bored after the scarph is bolted together. Stopwaters are traditionally fitted at all joints and scarphs reaching to the wetted surface and, being of selected softwood, should swell and prevent water leaching inside the hull if the scarph opens slightly, which may occur due to a shock, dragging along hard ground, or stranding. Today glued scarphs are often used and stopwaters are not then required, while the glue holds.

Given a sound crook for the stem, the scarph is more likely to fail by its fastenings than the stem to break across the grain. It is desirable to reduce the number of joints to make up an assembled member, and the type of scarph will depend on the fullness of sections at the forefoot and the radius of the stem at the forefoot; all of which will govern choice of a natural crook. In the average traditionally built dinghy hull it is arranged as in (23). The curved grain of the crook is short and can usually be obtained without too much searching. The knee, if not moulded too deeply, will not need to be too wide. When drawing out its profile it must be remembered that the width or siding is increasing much more quickly than the moulded thickness and its depth should therefore be kept reasonable. The drawing indicates a sensible length of bearing which allows adequate bolting arrangements. The end of the hog is housed and the joint can be easily clenched if a pair of bolts tying the stem to the knee are first set up or clenched, before the holes for bolts through the keel, hog and stem knee are bored.

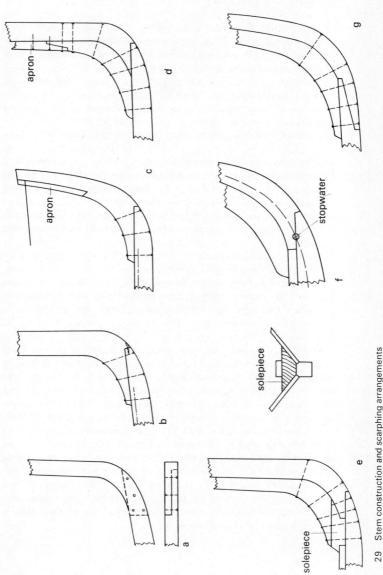

29　Stem construction and scarphing arrangements

apron

apron

c

d

b

a

stopwater

solepiece

f

g

e

solepiece

Preparation of keel and hog

The traditional form of keel (30a) is usually straight, but sometimes rockered. This is an expensive method of forming a keel, particularly if it is rockered and sawn from a straight piece of timber, when there is much waste.

Moulded keels are set out as shown in (30a). The spots are made on the stations from the sheer plan.

The most common type of keel construction in sailing dinghies is the longitudinally bent or rockered keel. Two principal variations of this construction are detailed in (30b,c).

(30b). Common in centreboard craft. The small deadwood is sometimes omitted but is an advantage for strength and to protect the keel; and may be used, in design, to assist steadiness on the helm and balance under sail.
(30c). The deadwood is fitted between the keel and the hog.
In both (b) and (c) a stern knee is illustrated as forming the sternpost.
(30a). A sternpost proper is fitted, half lapped to the keel. With this arrangement the siding of the sternpost is often the same as the keel and it is common to fit filling or cheek pieces to form a back rebate for the planking where this crosses the sternpost (30d); alternatively the sternpost is slotted through the hog.

If the keel and hog are rockered they must be bent separately before being fastened together or the fastenings will be distorted. They are bent to shape on the stocks, on which the station spacings are marked. The heights of the underside of keel are accurately measured above the upper edge of the stocks at each station on the laid off profile. Blocks are fixed to the top of the stocks to support the keel at those heights, and to avoid bevelling the blocks, they should be fitted on the side of the station line away from the fullest section of the boat—usually the midship section. Alternatively, a substantial mould should be made to the shape of the underside of keel, picked up from the laid off lines, and securely screw-fastened down to the top of the stocks; this is a more professional and firmer method.

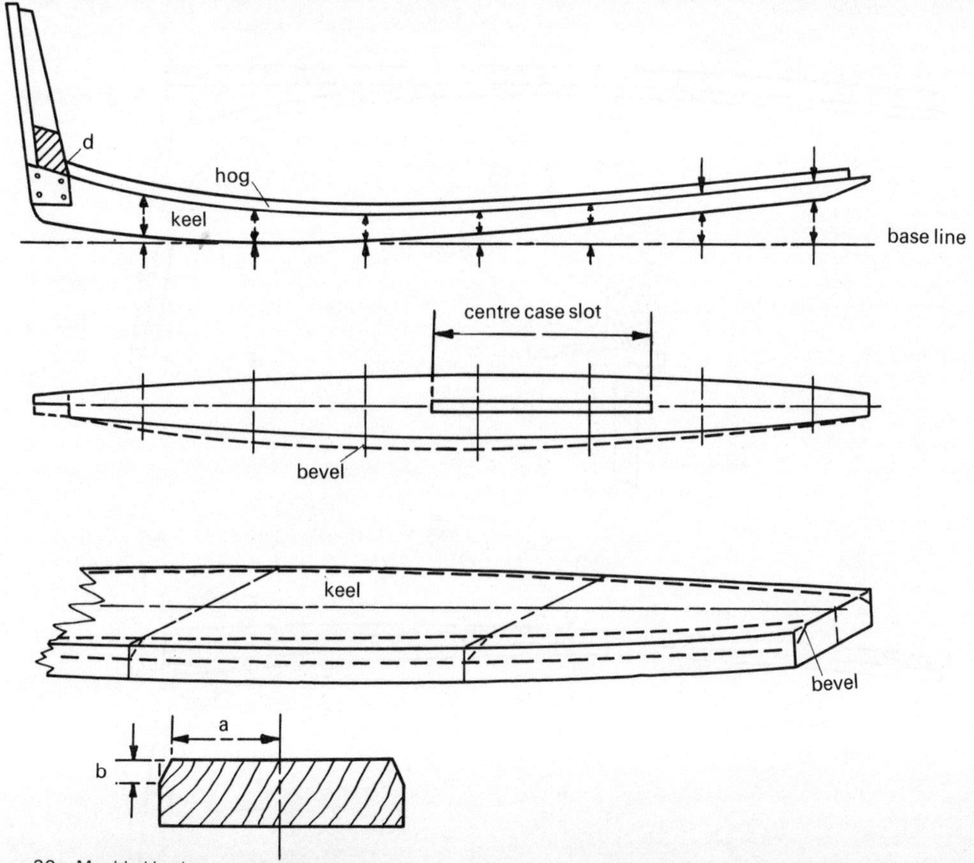

base line

centre case slot

bevel

hog

keel

keel

bevel

d

a

b

30a Moulded keel

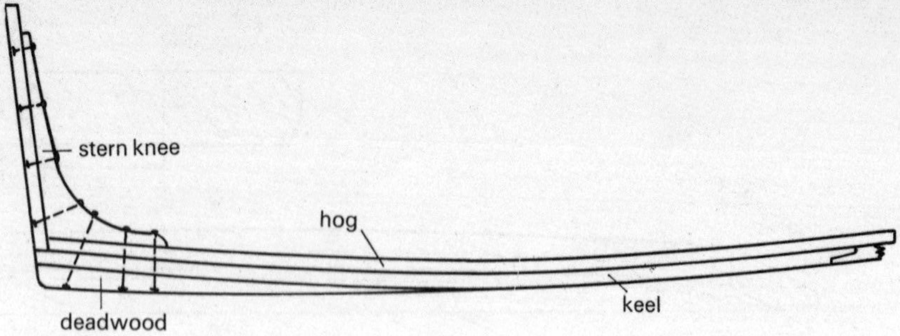

stern knee

keel

hog

deadwood

30b Bent keel with external deadwood

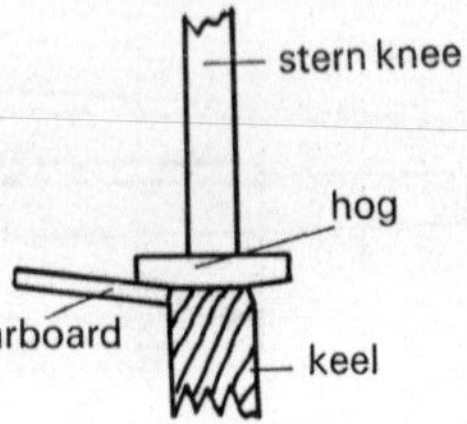

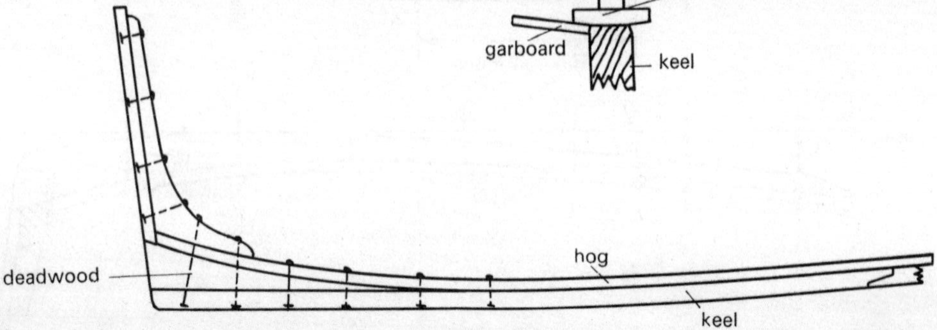

stern knee

hog

keel

garboard

30c Bent keel with sandwich deadwood

keel

hog

deadwood

If rockered, the length of timber for the keel should be carefully checked from the laid off lines as being adequate for the curved or 'expanded' length between stem scarph and sternpost, or transom. It should be sawn to approximate size

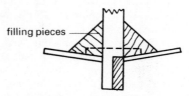

filling pieces

30d Filling chocks at sternpost

and be planed on its upper and lower surfaces. The keel should be laid on the keel mould or blocks fastened to the stocks and cramped down to the stocks, or be shored down from the rooftree with three or four light shores which should have small folding wedges under the lower ends to set them up.

The station marks on the stocks should be transferred to the sides of the keel by either a straightedge or a plumbob. These marks are squared across the top of the keel, which is afterwards removed and a centreline marked down its length. The easiest method of doing this is to drive a nail at each end on the centreline and stretch a chalkline between them, pull up on the middle of the line and let go. The chalk mark this makes on the timber can then be marked in with a pencil and straightedge.

The half widths of the keel on each side of the centreline at each station are picked up from the body plan and marked on the keel. The keel may be parallel sided, as in a rowing dinghy, but often tapers towards the ends; this is normal in centreboard boats where the keel will appear as (30a). These spots are joined with a batten bent round them and the fair line pencilled in. The keel is then sawn and planed to shape. Afterwards the bevels for the garboard strake rebate are marked out. These are indicated by the measurements a and b (30a) which are marked at each station and are taken from the full size sections of the keel on the body plan. It should be noted that b is not the planking thickness but a lesser dimension, due to the garboard planking usually being set at an angle to the horizontal. A batten is also bent through these spots and the fair line pencilled in (30a); the width of the keel has been exaggerated for clarity. The timber must be planed away to the lines.

The siding of the keel at the stem scarph will be equal to the stem siding clear of the rebate, otherwise there would be an

63

ugly unfairness. If the design of the boat shows the section of the keel to be tapered from the rebate line to the bottom this is also planed off.

If the keel is straight and parallel it is still best to work from measurements made from the centreline, as keels sometimes warp after sawing. Rockered keels are usually of parallel moulding (depth), but if any keel is of varying moulding this should be set out after marking off the station lines, as described above.

The centreboard slot can be set out, located from one of the stations (30a). The best way to cut this is to bore through each end with a large centre bit or electric drill, for about 6 in., and square the ends out with a chisel. The centre part can be sawn out, or could be grooved out with a plough plane; if a narrow iron is used the sides can be cut away and the centre wood will then drop out. The plough will leave a smoother side to the slot compared with a saw cut, which is difficult to clean up if rough. If a chisel and mallet are used to cut the slot, care must be taken not to split the keel with heavy blows.

The rebate at the stern of a straight keeled boat which has a tuck stern (or hollow at the lower edges of the transom shape) does not run out to the transom but is usually as in (31). The

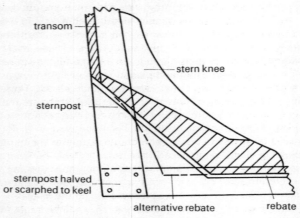

31   Stern knee and plank rebate for a tuck-sterned boat

64

planks get steeper as they go aft, tending towards the vertical across the aft deadwood or stern knee. It is easier to make this rebate a straight line, but it is sometimes designed as a curve.

The hog can be conveniently marked out by laying the prepared keel on a piece of timber of suitable thickness and length, clamping the two together, and scribing round the finished keel with a piece of wood the accurate width of the overlap which will form the back rebate; usually not less than $\frac{3}{4}$ in. for a dinghy, the general minimum being twice the plank thickness.

To mark the station lines correctly on the hog after sawing it out, it must be placed on top of the keel on the stocks and the station lines plumbed up its sides and squared across its face. The centreline is then marked on and while it is still in place on the keel a pencil can be marked round the edges of the rebate at the sides of the keel which will give the finishing line for the bevel to be cut on the hog to take the garboard strakes.

The outer line of this bevel will be marked on the hog at each station by spots taken from the body plan. To clarify: the line of the bevel which is to be cut on the hog is marked by a spot at each station and a batten is bent through the spots, the width at each station being lifted from the keel sections on the body plan. As the bottom line of the bevel is the same as the top line of the rebate already cut in the keel, it can be marked with a pencil while the hog is in position on the keel.

The bevel may run out to level amidships if the design is flat in the bottom. A bevel may be worked by plane, but a little extra should be left around the scarph, to be planed off when the scarph is made and the stem bolted on.

The centreboard slot must also be cut in the hog and this may be slightly wider than the slot in the keel, depending on the designer's construction detail. The making of the centreboard case will be described later.

The skeg or deadwood is fitted by finishing a piece of timber to the correct thickness and offering it up at the side of the keel, which is shored down to the correct curve on the stocks. The curve of the rockered keel is then marked on the skeg by pencil and the shape sawn out. The cut must be made square and should be sawn a little outside the line, allowing it to be planed to the correct line with a short plane or, if it is too curved, with a spokeshave. The faying surface to the keel should be tested during planing with a square to ensure an exact fit.

When the keel is of the type, with a deadwood between the keel and hog, (30c) the deadwood will have to be shaped before the hog can be fitted and marked.

Preparation of sternpost, transom and deadwood

If a stern knee is fitted it may be got out of a grown oak crook of the same siding as the keel or it may be laminated (30b, c). If grown, it should be roughly cut out at the start of building and be put away in a shady corner to settle itself, as grown timber for knees often warps badly after cutting and this will enable its final shaping to be carried out after this has taken place. Sometimes the leg of the knee which supports the transom is tapered in siding and on the forward face. Before cutting any of these faces, the aft surface which fays onto the transom should be cut to the correct straight line profile, which is best done while it is of even thickness. The shape is taken from the full size detail laid off on the profile. The surface bearing on the keel or hog will follow their shape and after scribing it out from their upper surface and cutting it out, the knee will have to be cramped to the keel or hog to ensure that it fays correctly. If necessary the surface may be chalked to locate the high spots, which can then be eased away with a plane. Both faying surfaces of the knee must be square, otherwise, if the surface faying to the transom was inaccurate it would twist the transom so that one side of the boat would be longer than the other. If the faying surface to the keel or hog was inaccurate it would throw one gunwale higher than the other. When the knee is accurately faced up the transom arm can be tapered at the sides, if desired, and the profile of the knee be finished with a spokeshave, rasp and glasspaper. The edges should be chamfered slightly and smoothed into the faces.

If the stern knee is also the deadwood (31), the first break of the rebate line is marked on it while it is in position. The lower part of the rebate is cut away but as it will not yet be certain how high the garboard strake will extend, it should not be cut too far. If the rebate is of circular form the width of plank is immaterial and the whole rebate can be cut. The datum waterline should be marked on one side and on the face.

If a sternpost is shown in the design, it should be similarly set out from a full size detail and the scarph marked, tried and prepared for boring for the fastenings. (31) indicates the position and angle of the scarph. This is set out on the keel by measurement from the adjacent station line or by pricking through a tracing laid over the timber. Great care must be taken when sawing the scarph and before cutting the line must be squared on all faces on which the cut will come. As the sawing progresses each line should be checked at intervals. The pencil line should be left on as it is simple to plane a little off but impossible to put back any wood. The old shipwrights' saying, 'Think twice cut once' is very apt here. After cleaning off, the waterline and lower rudder hanging position should be marked.

A transom may be vertical or raked in profile. If vertical, its outline is that drawn on the body plan and given in the offset table. If raked, its true form must be found by projection (32). The half transom shown on the design is set out to the left. Parallel lines are drawn across it to cut another line (y-y) which represents its depth and rake as shown on the profile. The lines are produced at right angles from their intersection with the line y-y and on them the widths of the original parallel lines x are marked, giving spots which are joined to obtain the true shape of the transom. This is its outline at the after face, outside the hull planking (the line c on the detail). A line drawn inside it the thickness of the hull planking will give its actual shape at d. The line required for sawing is the one marked e, which will be subsequently bevelled back to d. To obtain this, set out as many waterlines as cross the transom and project them on to the true shape (32). Then from the full size half breadth plan of the after end, the difference at each waterline for the amount of bevel (t) can be obtained. These differences, deducted from the waterlines inside the line c, give spots on the forward face of the transom. This is the cutting line. For the face which bears on the keel or hog a bevel can be obtained from the full size detail, and the curves of the forward and after faces of the transom will finish to them.

Pricking both curves through on each side of a centreline

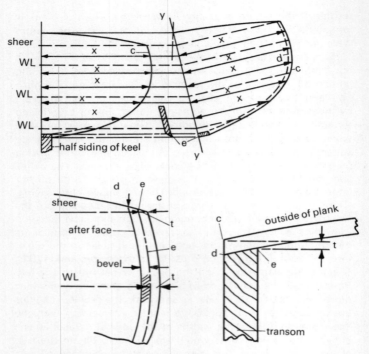

32   Setting out true shape and bevels of transom

enables the transom to be cut to shape e and bevelled back to the shape d. The bevel is a twisting one, being greatest at the sheer and smallest at the tuck. This marking out takes relatively little time and will save much trouble if carefully done.

Some amateurs and a few boatbuilders mistakenly cut the transom shape out with a large margin from the first curve found, and pare the edges to bevel as the planks are fitted, but even if the builder has good judgement and cuts near the bevel when sawing out, it is not simple to pare it down when the transom is set up on the stocks and is comparatively insecurely stayed during the early stages of building. It is well worth while to set out the actual bevels first, as very little shaping will remain to be done afterwards.

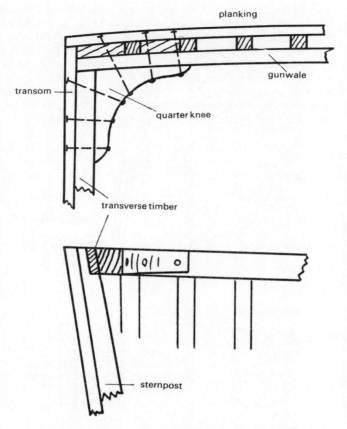

planking

gunwale

transom

quarter knee

transverse timber

sternpost

33   Transom strengthening timber and quarter knees

In heavier dinghies a transverse timber is sometimes fitted at
the top of the transom (33). This is really only necessary in
working boats and it is checked out in way of the sternpost and
is braced at each end by the quarter knees. If an after deck is
fitted it can be arranged to form a shelf or landing for the
deck planking. In craft for pleasure use the transom is
adequately stiffened by the combination of sternpost, quarter

knees and plank ends. The transom thickness will be indicated on the plans and generally varies from $\frac{7}{8}$ in. in a 10 ft dinghy to about $1\frac{1}{2}$ in. in a 26 ft boat. Unless it is exceptionally deep a dinghy transom can usually be worked from one piece of Honduras or African mahogany, iroko or English elm, which are the commonest timbers used today. If it is necessary to joint it, the joint must be horizontal and should be tongued and grooved very carefully. Alternatively it may be half lapped and the joint through-fastened with clenched copper nails, or glued.

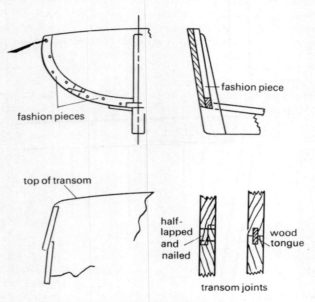

34   Transom fashion pieces, joints and top

If a very strong transom is required, as for instance in a boat to be continually driven by an outboard engine of considerable horsepower, wooden fashion pieces can be worked round its edges to provide additional bearing surface for the plank ends (34). Fashion pieces are often sawn from two or more pieces to achieve the correct curve and to avoid end grain. These are

70

bedded in and screw-fastened to the transom or may also be glued. It is possible to form a hull plank rebate by setting the fashion piece in from the transom edge for the thickness of plank, and the planking will then finish flush with the shape of the transom. If this is done, as it is sometimes for appearance and to protect the plank ends, the fashion pieces must be substantially fastened to the transom as they form the only bearing for the plank ends.

If the transom has a sculling notch, and all general purpose dinghies should have, this may be cut with a compass saw before setting up and finished with a rasp. Both faces of a transom should be cleaned off and glasspapered smooth, and the centreline marked lightly in pencil from spots left on the edges. The top edge will not be rounded and smoothed off until the hull is completed. Sometimes, for appearance and to protect the quarters, the upper edge of the transom is carried over the upper edge of the sheerstrake (34). This may be done by leaving extra timber at the top when sawing out, or cutting back into it when fixing the sheerstrake, to bring the upper edge of it into the transom which is afterwards rounded off to cap it.

Have described the working of the centreline members and the transom it is desirable to summarise procedure for their erection.

Laying the keel

Place the deadwood (if any) on the stocks and bed the upper surface. Place the keel on the stocks and align station marks. If there are separate fastenings to keel and deadwood, bore, countersink and drive screw fastenings, clench through-fastenings and set up bolts. Check heights at blocks, wedge keel with side cleats on stocks and remove shores.

Bed upper surface of keel and lay on hog. Align hog with station marks and centreline and shore down. Fasten hog with stout gauge bronze wood screws spaced about 6 in. apart, staggered in the grain. If hog has $\frac{3}{4}$ in. plank landings, the screw holes should be at least $1\frac{1}{4}$ in. away from the edge. Level hog transversely, adjusting wedges to shores if necessary.

Sternpost

Check the fit of the scarph. Bore keel for dowels, screws or bolts. Replace sternpost and mark hole accurately in it with a long, sharp scriber. The scarph fastenings will be best draw bored, i.e. bored slightly offcentre so that when the bolts are driven they will draw the scarph tight. The extent this is done will depend on the skill of the builder, but the difference is very small. With steel bolts it is perhaps $\frac{1}{32}$ in. and with copper clenches is less. The scarph is then bedded and fastened.

Transom

Transom to be cramped to sternpost. Check centrelines and tighten cramps Bore and drive fastenings, some of which may be bronze screws, but at least two should be through-fastenings of either copper clenches or galvanised steel screw bolts. One of these should be near the top of the sternpost and the other below half the transom depth. The transom should be checked for alignment with a plumbob and for squareness by measurement, as previously described, before being shored and stayed to the floor or the walls of the building shop.

Stem

Cramp together the stem, stem knee (if fitted) and keel. Check lines and stem with a plumbob, both transversely and fore and aft. The scarph may require adjustment in fit. If possible bolt the knee and stem together first, adjusting to marks. Alternatively leave cramped together. Mark knee and stem for through fastenings and bore holes for same. Scribe the holes on the keel at the scarph and draw bore (see sternpost). Bed joints, drive fastenings and clench or set up. If clenches are used the ends should be slightly rounded before driving. If screw bolts are used the nut should be well set up and the threads burred over afterwards to lock the fastening. A plumbob should be set up at the stem to check alignment and the stem should be shored both transversely and fore and aft to either the floor or the sides of the shed, but not to moulds, or in way of moulds.

Stopwaters

Holes for the stopwaters should be bored through the line of scarph and on the plank line, in the rebate. The stopwaters are planed from softwood to a tight fit. one end pointed, and they are then driven. The excess wood is cut off.

Moulds
It is best to adopt a set procedure for setting up moulds and the following is a practical sequence.

Place the amidship mould on its station facing the correct way with centreline located. Attach this to the keel with a wood cleat and stay it temporarily upright to a batten running from stem to transom. Tack two thin battens to the stemhead, near the sheerline, and lead them outside the mould to the transom, resting them on two nails driven in the transom edge, and tying them together with rope behind the transom. Measure with a batten from a spot on the centreline at the aft side of the stem to each sheerline mark on the sides of the midship mould. Swivel the mould until the distances agree, when it will be at right angles with the keel. Check the mould for vertical with a plumbob and adjust if necessary. When correct the mould is fixed by driving a wire nail through the batten, into the edge of the mould.

As all adjustments at this stage are tentative, the nails should be driven only sufficiently to hold. Set up and adjust all forward moulds by the same method, and nail to the battens.

Set up and adjust all aft moulds by testing distances each side of the battens, keeping the top spalls parallel and the moulds plumb.

Carefully remove the centre battens and tack a thin line from the centreline on the stem to the centreline on the transom at a height to just clear the top spalls of the moulds. Check the lay of this line on centres already marked on the top spalls of the moulds by a plumbline held by hand. Adjust the moulds, if required, by extracting the nails through the side battens and canting the moulds over until in position and then refastening the battens.

Move the line lower to lay on centreline marks at the waterline or, if the moulds are suitably made, lay a plank with its edge planed true along all the moulds to test for level. Unfasten any required to pack up and adjust, square and plumb vertically.

One adjustment often alters another and it is best to check that:

The stem and transom are plumb.

All moulds are plumb.

The amidship mould is at right angles and that all moulds are parallel.

All mould centres are on centre.

All waterlines are level.

Untie the side battens aft and nail them to the transom edges. Drive another nail through the batten at each mould and stay each mould from its outer ends to the rafters, if possible. If not, shore the side battens to the floor or feet of the stocks until one or two strakes are fitted. Tack another batten along the moulds around the turn of the bilge.

The moulds will now be fairly rigid but care must be taken not to knock or strain them until some planking is fitted. The moulds are tested for fairness by trying a thin batten along them in various positions. To avoid hammering it can be fastened to the transom by a bradawl and laid along towards the stem, being checked to see it lays fair against all the moulds. If a mould seems full, check it, if possible from the laid off dimensions. It may be found that the adjacent mould is not full enough. Find which is wrong and either pare off the fullness with a sharp chisel or fit a packing piece in the form of a sliver of wood which can be tacked to the mould and faired off.

Before altering anything check that the mould has not moved and is in its correct place.

The rebate at the scarph usually needs correcting and should have the bevels checked at each mould with a short batten about 2 in. wide, laid across the last two moulds and into the rebate, which is pared until correct.

If, due to mistakes, it is necessary to fit any slivers or filling pieces as corrections, these should be glued or screwed in place and bevelled off fair. If it is necessary to deepen the rebate at the forefoot the builder should be cautious of lowering the rebate line or undercutting it. There is a tendency to do both and probably spoil the fit of the garboards.

4 Planking

To plank a clinker-built boat so that all the plank seams are perfectly fair, sweet and well fitting is something of an art, but with patience it can be mastered by the amateur builder.

Thinner planking is required for clinker planking than for carvel because the double thickness of the plank lands, or laps, (overlap of the strakes of planking at the edges) compensates, while carvel planking must generally be thicker to hold caulking to make it wateright, which is unnecessary in clinker construction, except at the garboard seam.

A brief description of clinker planking would be that when the moulds are erected and faired, planking proceeds from the garboard strake which fits to the keel, working upwards to the

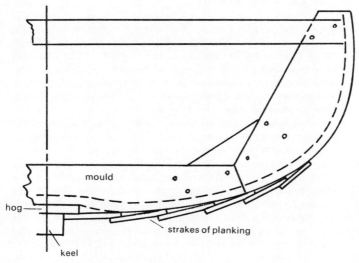

35   Hull planking on a mould

sheerstrake (35). The lands of the planks are nailed and clenched as they are fitted. The bent frames or timbers are put in after planking is completed; their position having been previously marked on the planking. The nails which pass through the timbers and the planking are driven and clenched after the timbers have been bent in the hull. At the turn of the bilge and where the shape of section demands it a soleing or bevel is planed off the edge of a plank to allow the overlap of the next above to fay properly to it. The width of lands usually varies from $\frac{5}{8}$ in. to $\frac{3}{4}$ in. At the rebate of stem and at the transom and sternpost the ends of the planks are rebated (the upper plank sunk into the one below it) so they lie flat on the stem, transom or sternpost.

The pram dinghy, with its transom bow which removes the twist from the forward planking, is an ideal clinker boat for a beginner; but a stem dinghy offers a better hull form and a worthy challenge to the amateur's skill.

Marking out planking

Thought and preparation are necessary before planking commences. The sweep of the plank edges at the overlaps or lands must be regular and fair throughout the length of a clinker built craft, where they are always prominent and do much to give the boat character and beauty as well as strength. Nothing spoils the appearance of a clinker boat more than irregular plank widths or distorted sheer of the lands.

As the largest girth of section is usually about amidships the planks are naturally wider there than at the ends. The number of planks on each side will be governed by the average width of each and the overlap given to their lands. Narrow planks are more easily worked than wide ones and in clinker construction provide greater longitudinal and transverse strength, but add to the weight and expense of a boat. The term 'average width of plank' is best used, as in planking the boat the widths will vary depending on the position of the plank relative to the section shape. Planks at the comparatively flat side and bottom amidships will be wider than those at the bilge, tuck or other sharper turns of section which require narrow planks to fit round the shape.

A pronounced sheer or a very small bilge radius will result in much edge shape or sny in a boat's planking. A hull with full body sections amidships but fine bow and stern will be more difficult to plank than a boat of normal form.

Hull planking marking out will be described in detail, but (36) gives a guide to how the curves of planking of a stem dinghy are affected by hull form while the plank is in the flat or developed state of being marked out; or alternatively how the planks of an existing dinghy would look if taken off the boat and pressed flat.

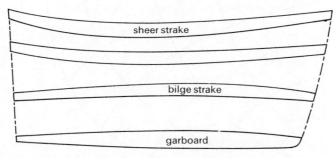

sheer strake

bilge strake

garboard

36   Hull planking expanded

A hollow bow and run in the stern usually result in the planking lands showing slight reverse curves when the plank is marked out on the flat board.

A transom sterned boat needs less work in planking than one with a pointed stern; the planking curves are easier and fitting planks to a transom is simpler than fitting to what is almost a second stem, as the planks are run by the transom and cut off after they are fastened. In the Scottish skiff type dinghy the curve at the pointed stern is often very full and needs much skill to stop the planks standing off from each other. Also, as the planks are restricted in length, a miscalculation in cutting a little too long will result in a plank sprung out beyond the others, or if cut too short a badly fitting end – though this could be eased by fitting a false sternpost and sawing the plank ends off flush with the true sternpost before fitting it.

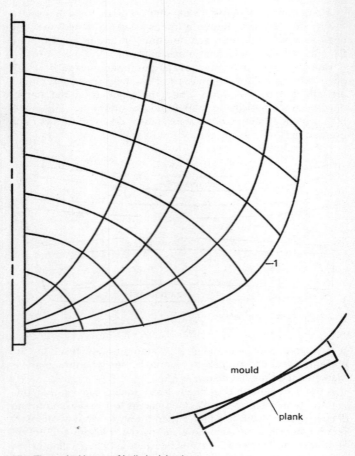

mould

plank

37   Theoretical layout of hull plank lands

The preliminary method of determining the width of planking at the various stations is shown in (37) which indicates the forward sections of a boat. The curve on station No. 1 is divided into a number of parts to represent the plank edges. The other stations are similarly divided and lines drawn through these

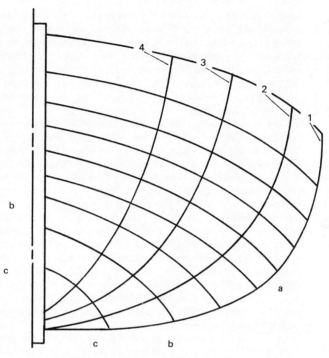

38   Typical layout of hull plank lands

spots with a batten will produce fair edges. If a thin batten is laid round these spots it would simulate the edge of a plank. However, the planking of an actual boat is seldom divided so evenly but is usually similar to (38). This is because the amidship mould has much greater girth than the others, and if they were all equally divided the planks would be very wide amidships and comparatively narrow at the ends. It is not possible or desirable to attempt to force a very wide plank around the curve of the bilge (38), and if the amidship planks are narrow the ends of the planks will be much narrower and their fastening will be a problem. Conversely, wide planks are very likely to split and warp. It is possible to have a moderately wide plank at b-b as the curvature there is small, and perhaps at the next plank also, and thereby reduce the difference between the amidship section and the other sections by using more of the amidship section curve than the others. The remaining space to be planked will not need to vary so greatly in width from amidships to the ends.

There are many ways by which plank widths are determined, but it is usual, before these can be settled, for the garboard (lc-c) to be set out, of generous width, at the amidship mould, and what remains on each station curve is then divided, allowing for narrower planks at the turn of the bilge. The setting out of the garboard edge will therefore determine the run of the remainder of the planking. If the boat has much sheer and the garboard is arranged to sweep up high forward, all the forward plank ends will be narrow and the planks will probably have considerable shape. An experienced boatbuilder will have little trouble in setting out planking, but the amateur must take great care at this stage of construction until he is satisfied that he has achieved the best possible layout of plank edges on the body sections. It will be useful to lightly fasten a batten where the garboard is to run and study the possible position of the edges of the other planks.

In small boats it is unwise to use clinker planking of more than 7 in. width for the garboard strake, and 5 in. is a sensible limit for other strakes, except the sheerstrake, which is considered next and should be a wide, sweet-sheered plank. On a traditional dinghy the rubbing strake to take chafe is fitted under the edge of the sheer strake, and to ensure that the strake below the sheerstrake appears to be of similar width it may need to be wider than the sheerstrake itself.

The widths of the plank ends above the ends of the garboard batten on the stem, sternpost and transom or sternpost, should be laid out tentatively by measuring the length of rebate above the upper edge of the garboards, remembering that some of the planks in the bilge will be of narrower width than average. If the planks appear to be too narrow the end of the batten may be dropped slightly, though it must still show a fair line. If there is ample width for the narrowest planks and the boat has much sheer, the batten may be raised at the ends. The amateur builder will probably need several trials with the batten before he is satisfied and it is worth taking trouble. When the batten is in place it is sighted carefully from various angles and heights to discover any unfairness and corrected by raising or lowering as necessary to achieve a fair line, which is marked on the moulds. A properly made fairing batten (described in Chapter 1) will naturally assume a fair curve when bent without being forced anywhere along its length. Often when a place is showing unfairness it is only necessary to draw an adjacent tack nail for the batten to spring fair. The batten supplements the boat-builder's eye for a fair line.

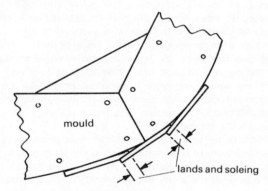

mould

lands and soleing

39   Lands and soleing bevel

A further check for the amateur can be made by setting out on, say, three full size mould sections through the boat, the full size widths and thicknesses of the planks whose edges have been determined on the erected moulds. This will confirm how the planks would lie on the curved shape and enable the bevel of the lands to be studied (39 & 35).

The points where the edges of the planks are to cross the amidship and other mould stations are marked on them with a batten and the widths of ends of the planks at the transom, sternpost and up the stem rebate are also marked clearly when the planking widths are finally decided.

The actual shape of each plank must be obtained before

cutting and it will be appreciated that, with so subtly curved a thing as a small boat, a plank which may appear straight on the boat when in place will be curved when laid out flat before fitting. Since planks cannot be edge-bent or distorted, wide boards are often needed from which to cut the shaped planks.

To obtain the true shape a spiling batten must be prepared from $\frac{3}{16}$ in. or $\frac{1}{4}$ in. thick pine, or $\frac{3}{16}$ in. thick plywood, about 7–8 in. wide and as long as the longest plank in the boat. This is usually less than half the plank thickness so it can be sprung from almost vertical at the ends to almost horizontal amidships. It may be necessary to make more than one spiling batten, depending on the shape of the planks. Some battens may be nearly straight yet will serve for most planks in a boat, but as planks assume more shape another batten approximating to this must be made. Three or more wood cleats about 12 in. long by 2 in. wide by about $\frac{3}{4}$ in. thick are also prepared. A hole is drilled through the centre and these are screwed to the keel; one amidships and at least one other midway between amidships and the stem and stern. These are used to give a grip for the nippers which will be used to hold the garboard strakes (40). A small cleat is also made and temporarily secured to the stem, just inside the rebate.

One end of the spiling batten is cut approximately, by eye and measurement, to the shape of the lower stem rebate and to the keel rebate for the garboard. The forward end is placed inside the cleat at the stem, and the amidship part of the batten

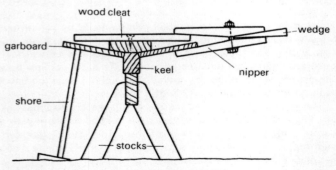

40   Use of wood cleat and nippers to fit garboards

82

is set in and held up towards the moulds and cleats on the keel. Nippers are than placed over the batten and the cleats and it may be further set in position by shores from the ground. A small wedge is driven between the cleat on the stem and the batten, to close it into the stem rebate. If the garboard is to be worked in one length the after end of the batten is twisted up towards the sternpost and is held there by a screw cramp. The batten may be laid up to the rebate but must not be forced edgeways, merely being allowed to lay on the moulds in a natural shape and be cramped to them.

Many boatbuilders prefer to make the spiling batten in two lengths, held together with an overlap in the middle by small cramps. This allows quick fitting at the ends, in way of the stem radius and the sternpost, particularly if the boat has a tuck, but the batten must be removed very carefully to lay it on the timber, or the two parts may move and result in a distorted spiling.

When bent approximately in place and to shape the spiling batten is carefully examined and the distances needed to make it fit into the keel, stem and sternpost rebates are measured and marked on it in pencil, usually at mould stations. However, it is better to set a pair of screw dividers to the widest difference between the edge of the batten and the rebate, and with one point carefully placed in the rebate, the dividers are held firmly at right angles to it and are drawn along the batten. This is termed scribing, as the line is scribed or scratched along the batten. A mark must be made on the stem, sternpost or transom and a corresponding mark on the spiling batten. This mark must be transferred from the spiling batten to the garboard plank when this is marked out and will locate the garboard when it is offered up.

When marking is completed the spiling batten is removed and laid on the plank selected for the garboard, to which it is temporarily secured by two lightly driven nails. With a fine pointed bradawl, holes are pricked through the line which has been scribed on the batten, about 3 in. apart. The batten is removed and the bradawl spots are scribed and joined by a pencil line drawn along a thin batten bent round them. This represents the lower edge of the garboard strake. The line for the upper edge is made by taking a number of widths of the garboard, measured at each mould and at the stem and transom, lifted from the marks made when the plank widths were laid out; $\frac{3}{4}$ in. is added to each spot for the plank land width (overlap for the next plank) and a batten is bent through the spots, faired and a pencil line drawn.

All plank edges should have a fair sweep throughout their length. If the batten indicates any hump or hollow when put round the spiling marks it should be adjusted to a fair curve. If necessary it is better to make a strake too wide rather than too narrow, as when tried up and found too wide, it can always be taken down and reduced, but if too narrow it will be useless.

When marking timber for a plank, avoid as far as possible knots, shakes and other imperfections. If the timber has no imperfections the strakes may be marked (41), and if carefully done it is often possible to get two strakes from each board, besides leaving a good sized belly piece (b) which may be useful to make a short length of plank or bottom boards.

41   Marking timber for planking

If the amateur builder is uncertain of his skill it is best to add a little to the width of the plank to allow for fitting the lower edge in the rebate. When the lower edge has been lined and sawn out the plank edges are planed fair with jack and smoothing planes and it is ready to be tried in place. This is done in the same way as described for the spiling batten, but it will take longer with the stouter plank.

The plank may be cramped to the stem providing a piece of scrap wood is placed between the jaws of the cramp and the plank, to avoid marking. It is usually best to cut some cramping pieces from scrap hardwood, to be fitted inside the stem apron/knee assembly to which they are temporarily fastened with steel screws. These may be about $1\frac{1}{2}$ in. square in section and provide grip for the cramps when pulling the forward end of the planks into the rebates. They are of course removed when planking is completed, and the screw holes are plugged.

The upward angle of the garboard plank throughout its length will depend on the adjustment of the nippers which will grip the cleats nailed or screwed to the top of the hog, throwing much strain on it. When a plank or a spiling batten is being fitted and the solid type of nippers are used to secure it, wedges driven between them and the outside of plank tend to give it an outward cant and vice-versa. If the wedge is on the inside of the plank it tends to turn it upwards and inwards. After it has been temporarily secured with nippers and shores it will undoubtedly be found that the rebate will need slight alteration in bevel to get the plank fitting snugly throughout its length. Some difficulty may be experienced in getting the plank to fit snugly to the first mould aft of the stem, or the first mould forward of the sternpost in a tuck sterned boat.

A sister plank is marked out and cut from the faired first one for the opposite side of the boat. A little extra wood should be left on this sister plank as the two rebates may not be exactly alike and the opposite garboard may require further fitting. A separate spiling may be made for each garboard if the builder is uncertain of his workmanship.

The garboard may need steaming in a steam box before final fitting, but if the boat has no reverse turn in the aft sections this is unlikely. In any case an adequate number of cramps must be available when fitting. It is usual to allow an additional $\frac{1}{4} - \frac{1}{2}$ in. on the width of a plank which is to be steamed, in case of springing or change of shape. If a plank has considerable twist at the ends and has to be steamed to achieve the shape, it should be given a twist by hand in the right direction at each end when removed from the steam box, as this will relieve strain on the nippers and end cleats when fitting. The plank is bent in place, cramped securely and fastened with nails and screws. If the garboard does not fit, which is particularly possible after steaming, it must be allowed to cool off and then be adjusted with a sharp chisel and a smoothing plane. The opposite garboard will probably need similar treatment.

In larger boats the garboards are sometimes worked in two lengths, usually commencing aft with a plank reaching about 2 ft forward of the amidship mould. The advantage is easier handling, particularly in a boat having a tuck stern and consequently much twist in the planking. A wider plank is usually fitted at the after end of such craft. Traditional boatbuilders commonly put set or twist into these planks by heating, as the steam box or pipe is not well suited for this work. A few shavings are lit on the ground and the aft end of the plank is held over the flames, hot water from a pan or kettle being sprinkled on both sides of the plank, which must be kept turning and wet. After a few minutes about 3 ft is steaming hot and can be readily twisted and secured in place by nippers and a cramp at the sternpost, being allowed to cool and assume shape, before the final fitting. When this is done a scarph is marked at the plank's forward end to join it to the other part of the garboard strake.

Scarphing of planks

Suitable lengths of timber may not be available for each plank in a boat and it is occasionally necessary to scarph two pieces to make one plank. Often in small, tubby boats the excessive shape in some of the planks makes it difficult to get them out of one board and scarphing is necessary. It is common to have to cut from a 9 in. board a finished plank only 4 in. wide in the centre, and economy is necessary for professional jobs or if material is difficult to obtain.

If many scarphs are necessary in a boat they must be arranged so that none of them are close together. A distance of 6 ft in length and three planks between should separate two scarphs on the same side of a boat which are in the same vertical line. It should be noted that plank scarphs are always set out so that the outside lip is at the after end or trailing; discouraging water from creeping up the joint face when the boat is going ahead at her fastest and ensuring that the thin lip will not catch on anything and tear open. A long scarph is stronger than a short one if both are accurately cut and well fastened. In dinghy planking $\frac{3}{8}$ in. thick, a scarph 3 in. long is adequate if it is arranged to come across a timber, to which it can also be through-fastened through the scarph centre, but a

length of 12 times the plank thickness is good practice. In
fitting a scarphed plank a line should be marked outside on the
keel or the plank below to indicate the position of the scarph.
The two parts of the new plank are then fitted separately in the
usual way; each being run a few inches past the scarph mark.
While each is in position the mark is scribed across them with a
straightedge. If the scarph were $4\frac{1}{2}$ in. long the after part must
extend $4\frac{1}{2}$ in. beyond the mark. The forward part must be cut at
the mark (42). The mark is not necessarily at right angles to the
edges of the planks, and when marking the saw lines on the
back of the planks it will be necessary to square the marks

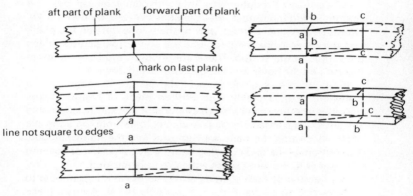

42   Plank scarphs

across the plank edges and measure the length of scarph at
each edge to ensure that the lines c-c are parallel to the original
mark. If this is not done the scarph will not be at the correct
angle when fitted together.

Professional boatbuilders can put a plank in a vice and with a
hand saw unhesitatingly cut a simple scarph which will have a
true face. However, the amateur builder should use a scarph
box. This may be made from two pieces of 1 in. thick hardwood
about 18 in. long by about 8 in. wide, nailed to a base board
parallel and vertical, about $\frac{3}{4}$ in. apart. A saw cut is carefully
made across the upright sides at an angle of 1 in 12 times the

87

thickness of the planking. The cut is made with a saw of medium set, carefully down the sides to stop on top of a piece of $\frac{3}{4}$ in. thick hardwood fitted into the bottom of the slot. The end of the plank to be scarphed is placed between the sides of the box and firmly held by small wedges. The scarph is then cut with a fine set, sharp saw working easily down the angled cut already made in the sides, which guides it to make a clean cut scarph at a constant angle.

If planks are scarphed and glued the plank ends to be scarphed must be carefully planed to a feather edge. The faying surfaces are coated with adhesive and brought together. If epoxy adhesive is used pressure is unnecessary, but the faying surfaces must be roughened a little with coarse glasspaper. The scarph is held in contact until the adhesive sets by two blocks, waxed so the glue will not stick to them, one outside the plank and the other inside, held together by one or two screws which pass through the scarph. These are removed after the adhesive has set and the holes are plugged with glued dowels.

If the scarph is glued outside the boat, one method is to assemble it on a plank, with a short piece of board on top, covering it. A few nails are driven through this sandwich to hold the scarphed surfaces in place and in contact until the adhesive sets. Afterwards the nails are removed and the holes plugged. The bottom plank and covering board may be waxed or covered with paper to prevent excess adhesive from sticking.

If a number of such scarphs are to be made it is also best to make a box jig to plane them accurately (42a). A cross piece and the front bear the plane to cut at the correct angle. A plank is secured by a wedge under the cross piece which is also used to set the plank so that the mark is parallel with the cross piece. As the plank sometimes has to lay skewed across the box, it should be made wider than the planks likely to be worked.

Traditionally the lips of clinker plank scarphs are fastened with copper cut tacks, about $\frac{5}{8}$ in. long. If the points protrude through they are turned over with a light hammer after being driven; the head of a roving iron or a heavy hammer being held behind their heads. Such scarphs are bedded on a piece of brown paper, sometimes coated with wet varnish, lead paint or tar, brought together with pressure from a nipper and a wedge or wedges across it to avoid hampering the nailing. However, a

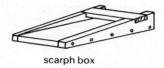

scarph box

42a Scarph box

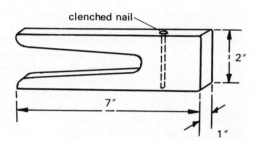

clenched nail

2"

7"

1"

42b Wedge clamp

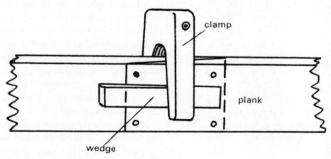

clamp

plank

wedge

42c Plank scarph closed with a wedge

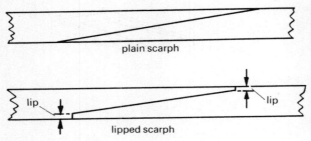

plain scarph

lip   lip

lipped scarph

43   Types of plank scarph

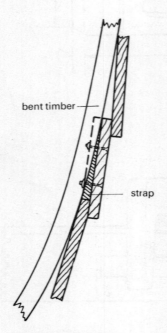

bent timber

strap

44   Rebated plank strap

mastic bedding will be better, or alternatively the scarph may be glued. Types of plank scarph are shown (43).

An alternative to scarphs, little used in small boatbuilding, is to fit a strap over the scarph inside the planking, between timbers. A refined variation of this which is now seldom seen was to fit a strap across the face of two timbers and between them in way of the scarph (44), fitted before the timbers are bent and rebated away to allow them to curve over it. In commercial work, or cheap boats, where a dead knot blemished a plank, a strap was often put behind it, bedded in thick paint and clenched to the planking. If the knot dropped out the boat remained watertight. Small knots are sometimes pinned in by clenching a tack on each side of them where the edge of the knot adjoins the wood. This prevents a leak if the knot falls out, but unless carefully done may start a small leak by loosening the knot. If in doubt the knot should be glued.

Plank lands

Before the garboard strake is fastened in place it is necessary to mark and cut the tapered plank end rebates, or bevels, to receive the next plank above. A line equivalent to the width of overlap or landing of the planks, usually $\frac{3}{4}$ in. wide, is scribed down from the upper edge of each plank to indicate how far down the next plank will overlap (45). The nail holes to fasten one plank to the next above will be in a line $\frac{3}{8}$ in. below the upper edge, in the centre of the land. As these lines need to be marked on each plank it is best to make a simple marking gauge to scribe both lines and ensure they are accurate

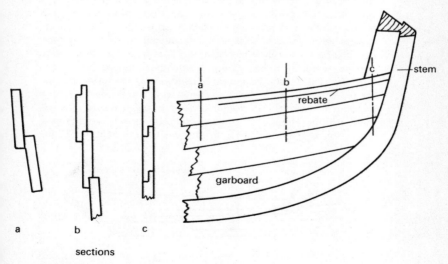

a b   c

sections

45 Rebate in plank ends

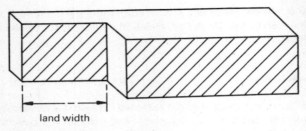

land width

46   Land or lap gauge

throughout. This lap gauge is cut from a piece of hardwood about 1 in. square and about 5 in. long (46). A pencil is held against the outer edge and the shoulder of the gauge is held firmly against the upper edge of the plank as it is drawn along it.

In clinker planking the ends of each plank have to be sunk into the plank below it either by a bevel on both of them or by a rebate which tapers out on the faces of the plank. This is done to avoid too deep a rebate and to achieve a neat appearance at the ends. It is shown in (45 and 48). Both methods result in twisting (winding) surfaces and it is not possible to get accurate results without some practice. The bevelling method is rarer and will be efficiently watertight, but is difficult to make and to achieve watertightness, though a skilled boatbuilder will find it quickest. The rebate is generally used and is the safer method for the amateur as if the workmanship is a little inaccurate, a bedding of waterproof mastic or lead putty in the rebate will make it tight. The length of plank end rebates will vary with the boat's form. In a fine-lined boat they will run out in about 12 in.;

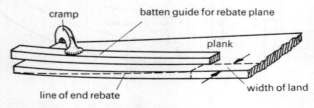

cramp   batten guide for rebate plane

plank

line of end rebate   width of land

47   Preparation for cutting hull plank-end rebate

92

dinghy may need about 7–8 in. and some full-ended dinghies only 4–6 in. from the plank ends. The length is measured and the gauge line gives the width of cut. As a guide a line can be drawn on the plank edge (47).

A $\frac{3}{4}$ in. chisel is a favourite tool for cutting these rebates, which is a job requiring care and thought. Much of it may be worked on the bench with a sharp chisel, having first made a saw cut longitudinally just above the line of the outside land mark. The depth of cut will taper from nothing at 12 in. or so from the plank end to the thickness of plank at its end. It may be difficult to get the bevel to melt off into the rebate without leaving a bump which would make the overlap of the next plank lie unfairly and cause a leak. It is best to get this bevel off by working a chisel across the grain. It is very important that the bevel should be flat faced and without bump or hollow, and each few inches cut should be tested with a straightedge until it is right.

The rebate may be planed with a short rebate plane, with a strip of batten cramped on the line as a guide (47), but if the plank is very curved the rebate will follow its shape and will require finishing with a chisel. If the rebate is planed straight by a plane too long to follow the curve it will show a hollow in the centre if the curve is concave, or two hollows at the ends if the curve of the plank is convex, when the plank is fitted. A steel rebate plane with an adjustable fence may be used, set to $\frac{3}{4}$ in. The forward end of the garboard is marked back along the gauged line an amount judged sufficient for the rebate and the

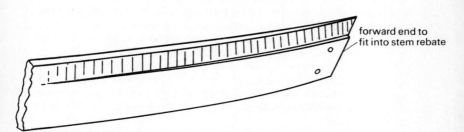

forward end to
fit into stem rebate

48   Hull plank-end rebate

rebate plane fence is applied to the edge of the plank and the rebate planed down on a taper from the mark down to $\frac{3}{16}$ in. thick at the lower edge (48). The plane must be gradually turned in the hand as the cuts are made so as to twist the rebate as shown. The rebate at the after end is worked in the same way but may need more care due to the shape of planking. The full depth and length of the rebate should not be cut away until the plank is tried in place so that the finished angle will fit to the bend of the plank. The upper nails in the end of the plank below the one being fitted should always be below the plank land gauge mark. If it is necessary to drive a nail above this during the fitting of the plank it should be driven with a piece of wood under the head so it can be easily pulled out before the rebate is worked.

When temporarily nailing a plank end the nail must always be driven inside the rebate, never in the side of the stem.

When finally fastening the wood ends in the rebate, the nails should be $\frac{1}{2}$ in. aft from the rebate line and the plank must be well bedded in paint, varnish or a waterproof mastic compound. Similar remarks apply to a pointed stern.

Sometimes the garboard is let into the transom, which is notched. This allows the next plank to lie flush on it and is thought by many boatbuilders to be a stronger construction, but may look ugly if used above water.

In small boats the garboard strake is usually fastened to the rebate with nails rather than screws, which are used in larger craft. The nails will be about 2 in. long and of heavier gauge than those for the remainder of the planking, spaced about 2 in. apart. The holes drilled for them should follow the bevel of the keel rebate so that each nail may be driven at right angles to it, if possible. The bronze ringed nails now commonly available as boat fastenings are excellent for garboard nails. In cheaper work the well tried galvanised nails hold very well.

If the garboard strake is made in two pieces the after part must be fitted to the scarph already cut in the forward part. This should not be done until both parts of the garboard are in place along the rebate as the scarph might move slightly while this is being done.

When both garboards are fitted and nailed the nippers are removed and the outer edges of the planks are planed fair and exactly to width as a pair. A 14 in. jack plane is useful to fair the plank edges. A slight radius can be worked on the inner edge and finger marks or other working blemishes are cleaned off the planks with a scraper and glasspaper.

Pencil lines should be made across the top of the keel between the after end of the stem or apron and the forward end of the stern knee or sternpost at intervals of the bent timber spacing, usually 7 in. These stations will assist in measuring equal widths of the garboard planks.

The amateur builder should not be too discouraged if his first attempt at a garboard plank is spoiled and has to be thrown away; the second attempt will be much more confident.

The land or soleing on the outer upper edge of each strake of planking, which has already been marked, will need to be planed away to allow the overlap of the plank above it to fit to it correctly. This bevel is planed after the garboard and each succeeding plank is fitted, and varies in amount and location, being more amidships than at the ends, and greatest at the turn of bilge. Usually it will not reach as far as the forward rebate but at the transom it may be necessary to modify the rebate with a chisel when the next plank is being fitted. This cannot be properly done until the bevel is taken off and some of it planed away before the plank above is tried, the remainder being planed off after the next plank has been tried on and the amount it is standing off the lower one noted and adjustment made. After a little practice the amount of bevel can be judged fairly accurately without measurement, but a guide may be made by holding a straightedge at each mould from the mark where the upper edge of the next plank above comes to the plank cramped in position (39). The amount of bevel can be marked by drawing a line on the upper edge of the plank at each mould, removing the plank and bearding off between the edge marks and the $\frac{3}{4}$ in. land (lap) mark. If these marks are planed near to, they will be close and when the plank is laid on for scribing the additional wood to be removed will be seen. The bevel should not remove more than $\frac{2}{3}$ of the plank thickness at the edge. If more is required it means that narrower planks should be fitted. If these land bevels are confusing at the start it might help to lay out two or three full sized sections at different parts of the boat with the planks marked on them.

In American lapstrake (clinker) practice, where wider strakes of planking are used than in Europe and Scandinavia, it is common for the soleing to be bevelled away almost to a feather edge to obtain a fit for the plank above. This practice may stem from the original American-built, European style boats which were often flat bottom types such as dories and bateaux, but which had sides clinker planked in a few, wide strakes.

Back soleing or bevelling of the land of the plank above to avoid bevelling away the lower strake to a feather edge does not appear to have been extensively practised in England, though it was used in Scotland. This should be unnecessary if an adequate number of strakes has been arranged, but it may be needed at the ends of planks in craft with a fine tuck stern or fine entrance at the forefoot.

A plank with reverse curve will need back soleing, an example being a plank running out where the transom meets the sternpost in a tuck stern. A lap gauge line must be marked on the inside, where it is necessary to back sole a plank.

Soleing is best done with a 6–7 in. long plane having a $1\frac{1}{2}$ –2 in. iron. Planing the soleing must be done very carefully and patiently. If badly fitted the boat may leak and there is no satisfactory way of remedying this. However, the power of taking-up of a clinker-built boat is remarkable and the most dried out or badly built craft usually seem to swell up in the plank lands after a few days' immersion and become useable; though this must not be relied on as a palliative for bad workmanship.

The strake next above the garboard will be easier to fit. The cleat on the stem is moved about 5 in. upwards and the spiling batten is laid around the upper edge of the garboard in a natural, fair manner, also touching all the moulds with its other edge. It is fastened along the upper edge of the garboard by nippers and a pencil line is struck along it defining the shape of this edge. The dividers are set at perhaps $5\frac{1}{2}$ in. or whatever width of strake is required from the mould marks, and at intervals of about 8 in. spots are marked on the batten in pencil to obtain the upper edge of the second plank. The batten is removed and laid on the plank for marking. Holes are pricked through as previously described, along the pencil line and at the spots. The batten is taken from the plank and the prick marks are joined fair by a batten and pencil lines drawn through them.

1   Sailing dinghy set up on building stocks. Keel, hog, stem, apron, stem knee
or fore deadwood, sternpost, transom and centreplate case clearly visible.
Note shores from roof. Keel securing cleats and wedges. Temporary cramping
pieces fitted inside face of apron and stem knee. Moulds omitted for clarity

2 Stem, apron, stem knee or fore deadwood, forward end of keel and hog; plank rebate in stem, back rebate and bearing line; scarphs of keel to stem and apron to stem knee clearly visible. Keel wedge in cleat on stocks. Temporary cramping pieces fastened inside faces of apron and stem knee

3 Garboard and next plank fitted and nailed. Third plank being fitted into stem rebate. Land overlap marked on upper edge. Plank held by nippers and wedges. G-cramp to stem with protective packing. Apron being cut to back-- rebate shape as work progresses. Moulds omitted for clarity

4   Hull half planked. Plank-end tapered rebate visible on land of upper strake. Temporary cramping piece screwed inside face of apron forming grip for G-cramp

5   Inside bow of hull completely planked. Taper of plank-end rebates visible. Plank land nails clenched on rooves. Bent timbers not yet marked or fitted. Clenched through-fastenings of stem to apron and stem knee visible. Temporary cramping pieces have been removed but cramp marks on inside of apron could be avoided by fitting a protective batten

6 Transom fastened to stern-post. Made in two parts with parallel hardwood tongue in joint. Sternpost halved to end of keel and clench-fastened. Plank widths marked in chalk on transom edge. Upper plank land rebated at end. Plank ends run by transom and cut off when fitted and nailed

7 Almost full sized detail of tapered and angled rebates of plank ends at transom

8 Bow fully planked, before timbers are fitted. Note position of reeled plank-end fastenings to apron and stem knee. Diagonal bracing shores cut over apron head

9 Completely planked boat before timbering. Stem bearded off to final section shape for full height. Hull supported transversely by light shores under plank lands and by shores from roof to apron and transom

10 Inside bow. Timbers bent and fastened. Wedges in way of fastenings under lower ends of two timbers which are bent continuously from sheer to sheer. Two forward timbers fitted to face of apron and fore knee. Gunwales and risings fitted and fastened through timbers and planking. Breasthook knee fitted and fastened through gunwales and sheerstrakes with packing between gunwale and sheerstrake in way of arms of breasthook

11 Transom and sternpost. Gunwales and quarter knees fitted and through-fastened. Packing between gunwale and sheerstrake in way of knee arms. Bent timbers continuous across hog. Hog screw fastened to keel. Amidship thwart fitted, with two knees on each side. Packing piece between gunwale and sheerstrake in way of upper fastenings. Further packing piece in way of rowlock chock position. Stern benches fitted on risings and let into after edge of thwart

12 Detail of amidship thwart seated on rising with pair of knees fitted and through-fastened to gunwale, sheerstrake and thwart. Stern bench let into after edge of thwart. Not evenness of plank land and timber nails and appearance of nail clenches on the rooves. Some hammer marks visible on planking in way of clenching

The lower edge of the plank is marked in at the width of the land (or overlap) below the line obtained from the upper edge of the garboard. When both edges of the plank have been sawn to shape the forward end is cut across to suit the bevel of the stem or stern rebate and the after end is temporarily left about 2 in. longer than necessary to let it into the sternpost rebate, or fasten it to the transom, to allow a working tolerance for fitting the forward end.

A sister plank is marked out and cut as planks must be fitted in pairs to maintain equal pressure on the moulds. One of them is planed fair and gauge marks are made along the lower inside edge and the upper outside edge. The upper edge is then rebated at the ends as described for the garboard strake, but the lower edge will differ. It is worked by a sharp smoothing plane. From nothing at the end of rebate mark the plane is gradually turned as it is pushed along so that a twisting bevel is cut, finishing at nothing inside, but at a $\frac{3}{16}$ in. deep nosing at the edge. This should fit into the corresponding rebate made in the garboard and.the rebate at the stem or sternpost, which it is best to make 100 degrees rather than 90 degrees to the planking so it is easier to fit the plank ends.

Care must be taken to ensure that the rebates are cut on the correct sides and edges as it is surprisingly easy to become confused in this. The top and bottom rebates should be cut in each subsequent plank before it is fixed and one is inside and the other outside. The upper plank at the stem is sometimes only bevelled where it fits into the lower rebate, but this is bad practice. There is a tendency for planks with considerable twist at the ends to split during or after fixing but this can be overcome by fitting a small supporting piece of wood across the plank, screwed through it into the stem or sternpost. This is removed before the next plank is fitted and the holes used for end fastenings.

The after end of the second plank in a tuck-sterned boat might be made wide to reduce the width of the two or three succeeding planks which will have to follow the hollow shape of the tuck. The after ends of these planks will probably have to be steamed or warmed over a fire, as previously described, to achieve the hollow shape.

The most shape will probably be in numbers 4 or 5 planks,

and it is often necessary to scarph one of these. However it is unusual to have to steam subsequent planks, so construction will become a little easier for the builder.

The position of the timbers will have to be progressively marked on the inside of planking at the desired spacing. This is necessary as a guide for drilling and driving the land fastenings, two between each timber, which are put in and clenched when each plank is fitted.

When fitting the second plank it may be found that special attention will have to be given to achieve the correct outward cant or flare throughout its length, particularly at the ends. This will also occur in the following plank. The nippers will need to be carefully adjusted as described for the garboard strake. If necessary, the set of the first two or three planks can be adjusted by shores down from the rooftree or from the building shed beams. It is impracticable beyond these planks as the plank edges rise and stiffen.

The outlines of the succeeding planks will be marked out and shaped much as those described, but they will become more curved, and wider boards are needed to cut them, particularly if worked in one length, which is best for strength. If a boat is big and beamy, often every alternate plank is scarphed, without much loss of longitudinal strength. A system might be to start at plank number 3 with a long piece aft and a short one forward, followed in the next plank by a scarph well aft of the amidship mould. Because of the inevitable shape in most boats it is preferable to obtain wood for planking which has a slight turn in the bottom of the tree. This is possible in woods like larch, elm or oak, but is unlikely in mahogany or iroko. If timber is being cut from the log it should be sawn to take advantage of any such turn in the butt. A tree wide enough to make boards which will cut two planks will be a great economy.

As planking proceeds, slight cumulative errors may occur after several strakes have been fitted, requiring adjustment in the plank widths previously marked, faired and lined, and if the planking is to be fair some of the upper strakes may have to be run again. To adjust the marks on the moulds is tedious but a well planked clinker hull depends on achieving fair curves on all plank edges, which in turn depends on the careful use of a fairing batten. Care is needed to maintain equal heights of the upper edge of the planks as they are fitted, and this is particularly important at the stem where any inequalities of the plank end heights will be ugly and noticeable.

If the planking has to be left uncompleted, as will commonly occur with amateur building, it is best to reinforce the edges of the plank last worked by cramping or securing a temporary batten along its upper edge with nippers. When the turn of the bilge is reached the plank landings will need to be considerably, bevelled to allow planks to get around the shape of the section. If the boat's bottom has much rise of floor, i.e. the bottom is not flat but rises outwards at a gentle angle from the horizontal, the bevel need only·be moderate; but if the bottom is flat, the bilge will turn at a fairly sharp radius and the plank lands will be bevelled off to a narrow edge for some distance amidships. This bevel is carefully assessed by eye after the plank is in place. It is first cut with a jack plane followed by a smoothing plane, both having fine set irons. Beginnning at the upper edge of the plank the bevel is worked down until it fades out at the plank landing gauge marks. The bevel reduces at the forward and after ends.

The planks for the bilge will have much curvature amidships, its amount varying with the beam and fullness of section of the boat. If possible the bilge planks should be in one length. If one has to be scarphed the join should be kept aft of amidships if possible. In offering up the spiling board or a plank it will be found that when the forward end and the middle have been secured to the preceding plank with one or two nippers, forcing down the after end of the plank, edgeways, always tends to turn the upper edge of the middle of it inwards, towards the moulds. The correct amount of inward cant can be judged and the spiling board fastened for marking by the nippers which, if they are of solid form, should be wedged inside the boat, which is the opposite way to which they were wedged on the bottom planks.

When the first pair of bilge planks are fitted and before the next pair are spiled the upper edges of the planks must be checked to see that they are equal in sheer height and in half breadth throughout their length. A light batten is bent round inside the top of the plank and is marked at alternate timber marks which are carried up the planking as each strake is fitted. These marks are tried on the other strake in reverse. Any adjustment to the sheer of the planks is made with a sharp and finely set 14 in. jack plane or a smoothing plane.

As the topsides are approached the lands need a little additional soleing and back soleing to ensure showing an even thickness of plank edges and to let the timbers bear in a fair sweep on the face of the planks.

The plank ends at the transom should not be cut off flush with its after face until they are fitted and fastened to it. These planks are rebated in the same way as described for the forward end for a distance of about 6 in. from the transom to receive the lower after edge of the next strake. The planks are worked wide or narrow around the transom to suit the shape where they fay onto it.

As pram dinghies have no stem rebate in which to enter the forward end of the planks, it is best to temporarily screw a block to the bow transom, to which the plank ends may be cramped while being fitted.

As the side is planked the sheer of the strakes lessens to the final sheer of the upper or sheer strake. These side planks are comparatively easy to work and are usually fitted in one length if at all possible. It is desirable for the top strake to be a little thicker and wider than the other planks, and it should be worked a little above the true sheerline to allow for final trimming to a sweet sheer.

Much of the detail of nailing the planking has been described in Chapter 1 and the following are supplementary remarks.

Planks must be fastened as they are fitted, all the way along, driving and rooving each nail along the land. No. 13 gauge nails and $\frac{3}{8}$ in. rooves are commonly used. If a boat has a transom stern this is nailed last. Screws are often used in the lower strakes but nails are preferable in the bilge plank areas they are being driven into the end grain of the transom. Galvanised nails are often used in commercial or plainly finished boats, but bronze ringed nails or screws are better, though the galvanised nails will hold for the life of the boat.

The position of the bent timbers will be marked on the planks as these are fitted and this determines the pitch or spacing of the intermediate plank seam nails. Usually there are two between each pair of timbers and the spacing should not exceed 3 in. An average spacing for bent timbers is 6–8 in., the intermediate fastenings being adjusted to space accordingly. A small batten cut to fit between the timber marks and marked with the nail spacing will save trouble in measuring pitch. Sometimes nails will come in way of a mould and cannot be driven until the mould is removed.

Assuming a plank has been fitted and is ready to be nailed, it is cramped in place with as many nippers and cramps as are considered necessary to get a good fit. The line showing the overlap will have been scribed on the plank below and the new plank is adjusted to this line. After sighting it carefully for accurate fitting, the first hole is drilled through the land near the amidship mould.

If nailing and rooving singlehanded, first drill the hole from inside, tap the copper nail in until its point just shows through the inside plank, place the roove on the nail point and hold it with the rooving iron in the left hand while the nail is driven home with the other, cut off the nail, hold the butt end of the rooving iron against the head and rivet up (13). After a little practice it should be possible for an amateur to nail and rivet a plank in about three-quarters of an hour.

If the boat has a pointed stern or a deep sternpost and the plank fitting is restricted at each end by stem and sternpost rebates it will be best to nail one or two fastenings each side of amidships, rooving each nail. If a transom stern it is best to work towards the stem from amidships, the other end being free. The plank will probably lie clear of the stem rebate. When within about 18 in. of the end free the plank from the rebate, if it is in it, but leave a cramp loosely on it about half way towards the stem to prevent it springing and the chance of the last nail driven splitting the plank. The fit of the plank end in the rebate should be checked. Rooving and clenching the nails which brings the planks together may make the plank stand a little closer to the rebate than when it was only cramped in position for trial fitting, making it a little too long. This must be trimmed off, but if left until the plank is almost fastened up to the rebate the plank end will not come out far enough to trim off. If this is not noticed and the fastening is continued, the plank will distort or cockle, and the lands at the end will not fit properly.

Nail fastenings should not be driven down flush with the wood surface but punched just under the surface, care being taken not to hammer the wood around the nail, as once this is bruised down with the nail head standing proud of the surface, the nail will not hold so well and may tend to draw. When drilling the nail hole the rake or slope of the planking must be considered. The hole must be started in the centre of the land, $\frac{3}{8}$ in. up in the case of a $\frac{3}{4}$ in. wide land. In drilling through the two thicknesses of plank, which may total $\frac{3}{4}$ in., care must be taken to emerge on the inner side in the centre and not on the edge of the lower plank. To avoid this the drill should be held as near at right angles to the plank surface as possible. Even greater care will be needed to drill through the two thicknesses of planking and the timbers, if this is done at once.

When drilling the stem or sternpost for dead-nailing the ends of the planks, care must be taken to ensure that the drill bit is marked to drill the depth of the length of the fastening, as copper nails and bronze screws do not enter oak very easily. If a copper nail bends when driving it should be pulled out as it cannot be straightened with success, which is often possible with an iron nail, and may lead to splitting of the plank end. Bronze ringed nails or screws are best for these fastenings.

Plank ends are liable to split due to their thinness and the rebating, so care must be taken in fitting and nailing. It is best to use two drills for screw fastenings; one of suitable size for the shank of the screw and the following one of about the same diameter as the core of the thread of the screw, allowing the screw to drive readily but hold well.

Hardening-up

A clinker-built boat, even a new one, which is leaky can sometimes be improved by holding-on and riveting the fastenings more tightly. Very light taps are best and more harm than good will result from trying to clench them excessively.

Reverse clinker

This is a variation in which the edges of the plank lands face upwards and all planks, except the first two from the keel are laid from the transom to the sheer, dispensing with the excessively shaped bilge planks. The garboard is the last plank fitted.

It is claimed that the planks are easier to fit as the system eliminates much of the twist and the planks lie flatter on the boat's sections, besides being straighter edged, crossing the bilge at an angle. The See family of Fareham, Hampshire, boatbuilders, did much to develop this form of construction in England, using it in sailing dinghies.

It is claimed that the outward facing planks provide additional resistance to leeward when sailing, besides additional lifting force, reducing wetted surface and allowing the water to pass outward instead of being trapped under the lands as in normal clinker construction. The most practical gain is that the boat is easier to clean out; a considerable advantage, as anyone who has cleaned and repainted the inside of a large clinker boat will appreciate.

More amazing claims are made for reverse clinker; owners stating they will sail to windward with centreboard raised owing to the type of planking increasing the resistance on the lee side and decreasing it on the windward side. At anchor in a stiff breeze they are reputed to heel to windward as the lands on the windward side pile the water under the bilge.

Reverse clinker is an interesting construction which might be worth trying for an enthusiastic amateur who has already produced a good conventional clinker hull.

Glued-land planking

Many racing dinghies which are clinker planked in plywood are glued but not through-fastened in the plank lands. The strakes are marked out and fitted in the conventional manner and particular attention is given to ensure accurate faying of the surfaces of the plank lands to obtain good bonding of the glue. The land and rebate surfaces are lightly sanded before the glue is applied, the strake is fitted in place, screwed to the stem rebate and the land nippered and cramped, working from forward to aft. After about 3 ft has been cramped together, small countersunk-head screws are fitted at intervals of about 12 in. to hold the land tightly together until the glue has set. The length of the screws should be about $1\frac{1}{2}$ times the plank thickness. Nippers and cramps are worked aft along the land in this way until the strake is in place. The work must be done quickly to be sure that the glue will adhere properly. The screws may be removed when the glue has set or, if of bronze or copper, may be left in place if weight is unimportant, as it would be in a general purpose dinghy.

Racing dinghies of glued-land construction are commonly built entirely without bent frames, but this is not good practice for a general purpose boat, liable to be often run ashore on shingle or manhandled down hards, etc. Plywood clinker is not too suitable for these dinghies as the edges of the planks are often subject to chafe and the protective coating on the lands cannot be expected to stand prolonged abuse.

5 Bent Frames

Fitting the bent frames or timbers, as they are generally called, in a boat is often regarded as difficult by amateurs, but is a simple task if properly approached.

A clinker planked hull can distort from its intended shape during timbering and must first be made rigid by an adequate number of side shores under the sheer lands, down to the floor. It may be necessary to remove some moulds to obtain more room inside the hull for timbering. If in any doubt as to the possibility of movement of the hull breadth, two horizontal spalls should be fitted across the sheer at about $\frac{1}{3}$ length from each end. Timber about $3\frac{1}{2}$ in. by 2 in. section is suitable, and vertical cleats should be screwed to these to protrude down from the side of the spalls to hold the breadth of the sheer rigid, inside and outside the sheerstrake.

Woods used for bent frames vary in different countries. In Britain, Canadian rock elm is a favourite; capable of being bent to small curves without splitting or breaking. Young growth English oak is also often used but needs careful selection as when dried out oak will go sare and tends to crack across timbers of small size in the turn of the bilge. Ash was traditionally used for boat timbers but is not durable and is prone to fresh water rot. In America, Canadian rock elm is an obvious choice. Newly cut white oak, if available, makes good bent frames and in Northeastern America, hackmatack is often good bending timber. Australia has a suitable frame bending wood in silver ash.

It is best to order sufficient quantity and length for all timbers to be cut to the length suitable for use amidships, where the girth is greatest, as some will probably be broken in bending to the bilge curves amidships and in the tuck, if the boat has one, and the remainder of these broken timbers may be used at the ends; particularly at the bow where the timbers are not carried from sheer to sheer but are butted or let into the centreline structure. The plank from which the timbers will be sawn is first thicknessed by planing and one edge is planed straight, in line with the grain. If they are to be sawn by hand a gauge mark is made down the straight edge, slightly wider than the desired siding of the timber. The first timber is then sawn out, the plain edge planed straight and another timber is gauged, repeating until the plank is converted into timbers.

However, it is now universal practice to have the planks for timbers cut on a circular saw or by a hand power saw and finished by a planing machine, to be delivered to the boat-builder ready for steaming. As timbering woods are tough and stringy they must be finished with a low-angle sharp plane where the machine has torn the grain. Timbers are naturally always prepared with the grain true lengthways and the scant-lings (dimensions) shown on the plans should be carefully followed.

Long timbers have a tendency to jump when being planed and are best held to the bench *behind* the plane, by a cramp. The length of timbers cut should allow for adequate hand hold above the sheer as well as the girth from sheer to sheer, amidships. Before bending the inner edges of timbers should be slightly bevelled or rounded off; about $\frac{1}{16}$ in. from the edge is sufficient. Apart from avoiding splitting on the edges this also prevents the boat's occupants from bruising themselves on sharp edges.

It is rare to fit timbers dry, but it is not always necessary to steam them for small boats. In the past, boats have frequently been built with ash timbers (though this wood is not recom-mended for durability), and ash up to $\frac{7}{8}$ in. by $\frac{3}{8}$ in. section can be bent around an average shaped hull after 24 hours soaking in cold water. Ash can also be bent dry, particularly if sprung round a template approximating to the shape of the sections and allowed to set on it for about two days, but soaking is an advantage as even if dry timbers fit well, the forcing into place may cause one to break after it is nailed and it is wasteful and annoying to have to fit another.

Water soaked timbers may be difficult to fit completely across towards the ends of a boat from gunwale to gunwale, particularly at the bow in way of the forefoot where the turn is sharp. After soaking in cold water the timbers should be wrapped around in the part having the most curvature with

106

absorbent cloth or sponge over which two or three kettlefuls of boiling water should be poured, rendering it much more pliable. Alternatively, the timber can be bent and weighted down into a pan or tray which can be filled with boiling water to achieve pliability.

Where it is desired to use gradual bending it is best to cut a rough template rather than rely on heavy nails or blocks nailed to the floor to obtain the shape. The template is fastened to the floor and the timber is less likely to break as it has a surface to bear against constantly. Timber can be bent to acute shapes providing the shape is even throughout its length, but any sudden turn causes all the stress to collect at that spot and the timber cripples and breaks.

An alternative to these methods and the most commonly used form of preparation for bending the bent frame timbers is to use a steam box or pipe in which they are steamed or boiled. An inexpensive and crude form used by many small yards and amateurs is shown in (49). A length of cast iron or steel pipe or fabricated sheet metal having a minimum internal diameter of about 6 in., has one end sealed with a welded cover plate or a

49   Elementary steaming/boiling pipe

softwood plug which is driven in tight with a piece of rag as caulking. The wood plug, kept wet by water inside the tube, will not burn but may char, and the lower end of the tube should be sunk into the ground to avoid the fire; the upper end being supported by a crutch (49). A fire is built under the lower end, confined by a few bricks, and a plentiful supply of scrap wood must be prepared as it is surprising how quickly fuel is consumed when steaming a set of timbers. Alternatively, a bottled gas flame can be played on the tube, which should be about two-thirds filled with water. The disadvantages of this method are that it will steam only a few timbers at once, and if the fire is too fierce it will shoot water out at the top of the tube, though this and heat loss can be reduced by wrapping a wet sack over the top opening. If short timbers are being steamed it is best to tie a string to the end of each to aid withdrawal from the tube without scalding.

An alternative device for boiling boatframes (50) was devised by John Gardner, mentor of the resurgence of American recreational boatbuilding as technical editor of *National Fisherman* magazine—a mine of practical information on materials, methods and supplies for the modern wood boatbuilder. This boiling box can be used in a boat shop adjacent to the construction, as it is a clean method. Heat is applied by a propane gas soldering or blow torch to a short length of 3 in. diameter copper tube which is inserted in the bottom of the long, narrow wooden box. This is securely fastened in a vertical position and is open at the top to receive water and the timbers to be

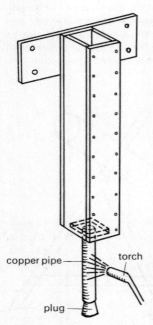

copper pipe

torch

plug

50   Gardner type boiling box

boiled. The tube is plugged at the lower end. Once the water in the box is heated an occasional flash from the torch against the tube will maintain the water at boiling point. A simple steam box or kiln can be made from timber and will last for many years (51). This is best made from four pieces of pine, about 7 in. by $\frac{3}{4}$ in., 8 ft long. Alternatively, it should be sufficiently long to accept the longest timber to be steamed. The rear end is closed in and the box must be nailed and bedded together at the joints with mastic bedding. The boiler may be an old 10 gal. oil drum, kept about two-thirds full of water and connected to the box by

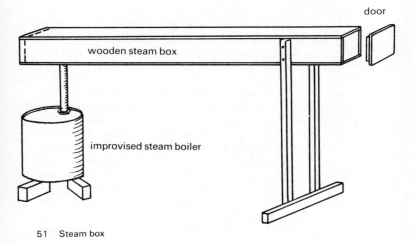

51   Steam box

a 1 in. bore pipe fitted tightly in the hole of the drum and led to a hole in the box, as detailed. The box should be supported at each end by two nailed-on legs with a foot across the bottoms. The front end has a removable or hinged lid which is made tight with rag, but a certain amount of steam leakage is expected. This type of steamer does not, of course, hold any water, though some will condense in it. The boiler should stand on some bricks and a fire be built around it, or a gas flame be played on it. For a small steam box up to say 4 in. square by 6 or 7 ft long, for steaming timbers of small section, steam can be supplied by a Primus stove heating a large tin kettle or by an electric kettle, having a rubber or plastic pipe led from its spout to the steam box.

The correct amount of steaming can be found by trial but it should always be remembered that the less a timber is steamed the longer it will last. Half an hour is usually sufficient for small boat timbers. Longer periods extract some of the natural juices from the wood and may make it brittle and quick to decay. However, some timbers may need as much as $2\frac{1}{2}$ hours' steaming to make them sufficiently pliable.

The positions of the timbers must be marked on the inside of the planking to ensure that they will be upright and evenly spaced. In a clench-built boat the timber positions will have been marked when the plank lands are nailed, as the fastenings between the timbers have to be spaced and nailed as the planking proceeds.

However, before the timbers are bent into the boat, their positions must be accurately marked inside the boat. A batten having the same width (siding) as the timbers and about $\frac{1}{8}$ in. thick is bent down one side of the inside of planking amidships, in the position of a timber, and is carefully plumbed at the head and adjusted to be exactly at right angles to the boat's centre-line. This is very important as misaligned timbers mar the appearance. A light pencil line or a scribed line is then drawn along each side of the batten, down the planking. This is repeated at spacing intervals on each side of the boat. After-wards, a drill bit of the correct size to suit the timber nails is used to bore a hole through each land in way of the timber, drilling from the *inside*, midway between the markings repre-senting the sides of the timbers. A nail is then placed in every hole on the outside. These are driven lightly in so that the points do not come through inside, ready for driving up through the timbers while they are hot. These nails should not be less than $1\frac{1}{2}$ in. long, and if possible of rather stouter gauge than those through the planking.

Where the shape of section of the boat is such that the timbers cannot be bent continuously across the hog and keel from gunwale to gunwale, the lower ends must be let into accurately marked and cut pockets, of the same size as the section of timbers and cut into the keel, hog, deadwoods or stem before timbering commences.

Two light shores of sufficient length to reach from the rooftree to the bilge, and four wedges, will be useful for forcing down and securing timbers in place until a few nails are driven. If the timbers have been properly steamed the nails will easily drive up through them without boring. The heavy end of a rooving iron or the head of a large hammer must be held inside, by an assistant, on the timber just clear of where the nail will pierce through it.

Before commencing timbering check that all tools and shoring and cramping aids are prepared, and that the kiln has plenty of water, fuel or gas. A stout pair of old gloves may be an advantage for amateurs when holding hot timbers, and anyone working inside the boat must wear soft shoes or slippers.

Timbers are usually fitted amidships first, working along to the ends. With a helper inside the boat bending the timber, the lower end is held in place near the hog or keel by the right knee or foot and the upper end is firmly grasped in the left hand with downward pressure, while the middle part is forced home into the turn of the bilge. While bending, the head of the timber should be held inboard, giving it a sweep and letting it back against the plank lands gradually as the outside helper drives the nails. The man inside holds on the timber, with a 4 lb hammer adjacent to the nail.

Timbers at the ends of a boat must each be given edge bend to stretch the longer edge. As the head is set inboard it is also bent forward, in timbering the forward part of the boat, to stretch the *aft* edge and obtain the necessary bevel. The timber is bent slowly and carefully into the boat; if possible, one man taking one side and one the other. When the timber is well down in each bilge a G cramp is secured at each head, cramping the timber to the sheerstrake. A nail (often a galvanised one in professional building) is driven in the centre of the timber to hold it steady on the hog. With the timber quickly checked to see it is fair to the marks inside the planking, the nails are ready to be driven while the timber is still hot. One man inside holds a heavy dolly, hammer head or weight on top of the timber close to the garboard land nail, which is then driven up through the planking and timber by quick hammer blows from the man outside. The nail should drive easily through the timber without splitting it. Working up from the garboard, each nail must be driven well home and the man holding on inside follows along holding behind the timber close to each nail being driven. When the turn of bilge is reached the G cramp may be removed from the sheerstrake so that the timber will fit down snugly into the bilge, the nails successively drawing it down as they are driven. This process is repeated with each timber until all are complete. It is essential to work quickly to drive all nails while the timbers are still hot. Nails are usually driven through a steamed timber without drilling, but unless it is well steamed it may be found that the nails are splitting it and holes must then be drilled through the timber by passing a drill through the holes already drilled in the planking. The nails must have the heads driven in flush to the surface of the planking and in harder woods will need to have slight countersinks made.

If the nails are all driven but not rooved as timbering progresses, they should be rooved and clenched as soon as possible afterwards to ensure the timber fits snugly down on the planking.

If no help is available it is best to place a heavy weight carefully across the timber adjacent to the nail, which will hold it firmly while the nail is driven from below. When the first three or four are driven it will probably be necessary to free the sheer cramp and work the timber a little further down to fit the following lands.

An alternative method of fastening the timbers is to turn the nails as described in Chapter 1, but rooving is recommended for the amateur. In boats with considerable shape of section or where appearance of finish is unimportant, the timbers are sometimes more easily bent in pairs from each gunwale down, overlapping alongside each other across the hog and keel. This is often done in working craft to strengthen the bottom.

When a centreboard is fitted the timbers are carried across the slot and cut away afterwards. They should be nailed to the hog or keel on each side, the nails being kept clear of the centreboard case sides to avoid need of removal when the case is fitted. The sills of the case will be fitted over the heels of the timbers.

The last few timbers at the bows or in a tuck-sterned boat will almost certainly need to be cut at the keel and stem or sternpost as it will not be possible to bend them continuously around the acute curves. Also, due to the angle the planking makes with the centreline, it will be necessary to twist them sideways to lay flat on the planking. In boats with very full, round bows several of these timbers may be fitted on the cant, or radiating from the centreline to lie fair with the planking.

The thickness of the hog will keep the timbers off the garboard and possibly an adjacent plank for a short distance (52), leaving a triangular gap. Wedge-shaped filling pieces are usually fitted if the gaps are extensive, but a limber hole must

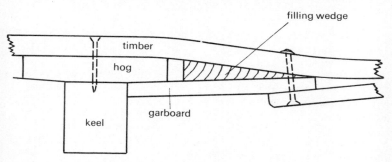

52   Timber heel filling wedges

be left beside the hog for drainage. Limbers should be fairly large as otherwise they will soon choke with dirt and silt; $\frac{3}{4}$ in. is a reasonable width for a dinghy.

The upper ends of the timbers are left standing above the gunwale until this is fitted and fastened. Then it is easy to saw them off flush.

If sawn frames are to be fitted in a clinker boat, as they often were in working craft and early yachts, this is done after planking is complete. The shape of frame must be lifted from the inside of the hull by a template of thin wood. This is applied to a piece of timber, usually oak or acacia, having similar grain configuration to the curve of the hull, and the shape is sawn out. The frame must fit closely to the inside of plank and is notched over the lands, if possible leaving a small limber

113

opening in the corner. The surface faying to the plank will be bevelled to suit the hull curves.

It will probably be impossible to obtain a piece of timber which will make a frame from the sheer to the keel, and it will be necessary to butt the parts (probably two in a small boat) together and connect them with a butt strap of similar siding, and length 12 times the siding, through-fastened to the parts of the frame. The heel of such frames is usually fastened to a floor.

Sawn frames and floors are now usually only needed in clinker working boats such as oyster skiffs, dredger or mooring boats, and fishing boats, but are still sometimes fitted in yachts as a ground for a bulkhead.

6 Centreboards and Daggerboards

A centreboard, centreplate or daggerboard is fitted to a boat to improve the hull's ability to sail to windward, by providing adequate yet variable immersed lateral area. Centreboards or centreplates lower or lift on a pivot bolt at the forward lower corner and are usually kept permanently in the centrecase when not in use. Daggerboards are generally narrower, sliding vertically, and made of wood and sometimes of steel, aluminium alloy or bronze. They are usually withdrawn from the case after use.

Centreboards are made of wood; centreplates usually of steel but also of aluminium alloy or bronze. Because of their greater thickness for strength, wooden centreboards need a wider slot in the consequently greater keel siding. A narrow width centreboard may be made from one piece of hardwood.

Dinghy centreboards or daggerboards are now commonly made of marine plywood, but care should be taken in its selection. When a boat is under sail, particularly in a hard breeze, there is a side force on a centreboard or daggerboard causing bending. The effect of this is concentrated where the board emerges from the slot in the hull. If made of ordinary marine plywood, less than half of the usual five veneers have vertical grain and the cores are made of light timber, giving poor resistance to bending. It is possible to obtain bend-resistant marine plywood specially made for centreboard or daggerboard construction by having seven or nine laminations of hardwood, five of which are vertical in grain. This is usually made in sheets 8 ft by 3 ft. The seven laminations type is 12—15 mm thick and the nine laminations type 18 mm thick.

Centreboard case construction

A centreboard case may be fitted either before or after planking is complete. If before, the moulds in way of it will have to be made with recesses to clear the case, unless it is short

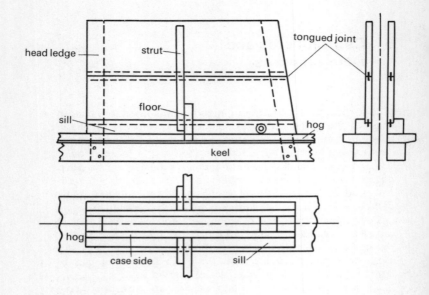

head ledge

strut

tongued joint

floor

sill

hog

keel

hog

case side

sill

54 Headledges slotted through keel

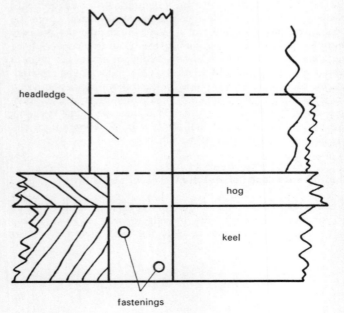

headledge

hog

keel

fastenings

enough to fit between two moulds. Moulds which are recessed can be attached temporarily to the case by wood cleats screwed to the case sides. The case is much more easily fitted when the keel and hog are being assembled and this is the usual method.

Typical construction of a centreboard case is shown by (53), whatever its profile shape may be. The headledges are often of oak; the case sides of mahogany or good quality spruce or pine. Iroko can also be used for the case sides, sills and headledges. Any joints of the sides, or of the sides to the sills, should be tongued and grooved or made with softwood splines driven in them.

The headledges are arranged to pass through the ends of the slot in the hog and keel, sometimes totally and often shouldered down. The slotted-in part of the headledge is through-fastened to the keel, horizontally with screws or copper clenches (54).

The sill pieces attach the sides of the case to the hog and are intended to accept the wringing strains on the case. There are several ways of arranging the sills (55a–e). The commonest and worst (a) is when the case sides are simply placed on top of the hog and are fastened with screws up through the keel and hog into the bottom edges of the case sides, backed up with a sill which is through-fastened to the hog and keel and before fitting is screw-fastened to the case sides. The watertightness of this arrangement is dependent on the fitting of the simple joints and their bedding but is liable to racking and leaks—an arrangement often seen in cheaply built boats but one to avoid. A better arrangement is (55b) and is an improvement and commonly used by good professional boatbuilders but is not fully leakproof. It is not easy to obtain a fit of the case bottom edge and side where these fay onto the rest of the structure because the rebate for the sides will have to be cut in the keel and hog before this is assembled.

If types a, b or c of case construction are used the sill pieces may be fitted after the case sides are bedded and screw-fastened from below. The side screw fastenings through the sills are fitted next and the clenches or screw bolts fastening the sills through the keel and hog last, pulling the case down firmly and probably requiring the vertical, case screw fastenings to be further hardened-up.

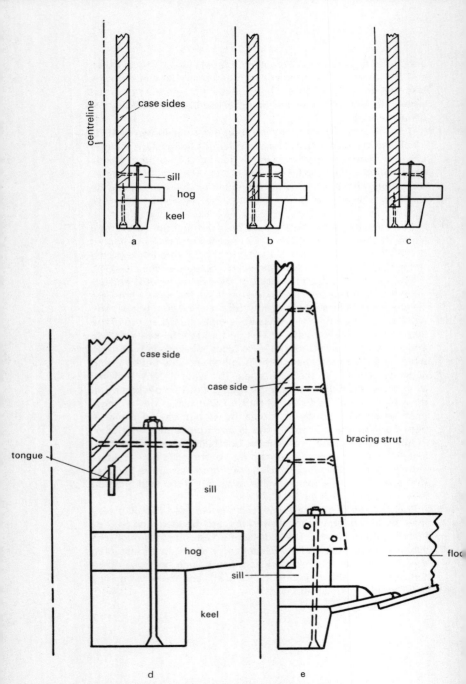

55a-e Various arrangements of centreboard case sill construction

The most certain method, which inevitably involves most work, is d. Heavy sill pieces are bolted through the hog and keel and have sufficient width to be stable. The case sides are rebated into them and additional watertightness is obtained by softwood tongues driven into rebates worked in the sills and case sides. The sills are carried to the forward and after faces of the headledges, to which they are through-fastened. The case sides are copper-clenched to the sills; the nail heads being inside the centreboard case, permitting them to be held against if ever they need be hardened-up in future.

Screws are not recommended to fasten case sides to the sills as, however well constructed, all centreboard cases tend to move or work slightly when sailing with the plate lowered, and sometimes when the boat is lying awkwardly aground. Copper fastenings are elastic enough to withstand these strains and, being clenched, cannot work out, which wood screws will tend to do. If screws are used they should be of bronze and always driven from the *outside* of the sills into the case sides. They can then be hardened-up if required.

Marine plywood is now frequently specified for centreboard case sides, but this cannot be rebated for tongues and is a questionable material for craft likely to be kept afloat for long periods, when the hidden edges of the plywood case will tend to delaminate, particularly in the frosts of winter. It is preferable to use well seasoned timber, thick enough to be rebated for the tongues and to be half-lapped where jointed to the next piece fitted above it to form the case side. Traditionally, many centreboard case sides made in more than one piece had the lower part thicker than the upper, to rebate out and cover the joint, but this practice is out of fashion.

Some high-class racing dinghies whose heavy metal centre-plates imposed strain on the case in a longitudinal as well as transverse direction were strengthened as in (56). The lower part of the case sides was carried forward and aft beyond the headledges, and the space between, the thickness of the headledges, filled with soft wood chocks. The sides and chocks were through-fastened horizontally and the chocks vertically to the hog and keel.

It was common practice to fit a knee at each end of the centreboard case to ease the change of longitudinal strength

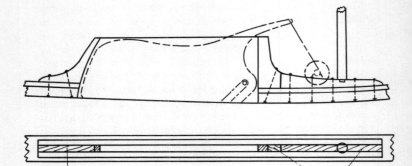

chock

rhnnke

56   Racing dinghy centrecase, traditional construction

from the rigid centreboard case to the possibly more flexible
keel, but this should be unnecessary in small boats. The knees
were fayed up to the headledges on the forward and after faces
and to the top of the hog, and were fastened to these with stout
screws.

In general purpose boats the centreboard case should be
transversely supported by a thwart or, if that cannot be
arranged, by a pair of large knees fitted in way of the position of
the shoulder of the plate when lowered. A further and now
common alternative is to fit a pair of struts on the sides of the
case in that position and shoulder their lower ends to a floor,
fastening to the case sides with screws and to the floor with
two bolts (55e).

These principles were ignored in most of the beautifully built,
clinker planked, one-design racing classes which flourished in
many countries before plywood and then plastic came to
dominate racing dinghy construction. The boats usually had
centreboard cases as type a but with no permanent thwart to
brace the case top. A class of 18-footers, one of which the
author owned and raced, have only removable half-thwarts on
each side, fitting into chocks on the case and the risings; and
these are usually removed when racing for greater accessibility
in the cockpit. The heaviest type of cast steel centreplates are
fitted, yet in ordinary summer racing for many years the case

120

construction rarely leaked, although it moved considerably in a transverse direction.

Setting out

The centreboard case sides and headledges are set out full size on the profile of the lines, perhaps in coloured chalk, and the dimensions are marked out on the timber. The headledges should have an adequate tail to pass through the hog and keel. The sides are made square to the bottom if the case is made as in d. If made as a, b, c, or e, sufficient must be left on the bottom for it to be fitted to the shape of the top of hog. To obtain this a thin piece of waste board or plywood is cut to the length of the case slot and held inside it against the side. A pencil line along the top of the hog gives the shape. This is planed down carefully and makes a template from which the sills or the case bottom can be marked before being cut, planed and tried separately to the hog to ensure an accurate fit. The headledges must also be carefully fitted to the top of the keep, if constructed as b.

The case sides are first fastened with temporary screws to the headledges, care being taken to ensure that the sides are level at the bottom or the case will not seat correctly to the sill or the hog. The sides are then bedded and clenched to the headledges and the hole for the centreplate bolt is bored through the sills with its centre level and square to the boat's centreline. The faying surface of the underside of the sills to the hog must be particularly well bedded, and it is common practice to lay two strands of caulking cotton in the bedding on top of the hog, before the box sills are lowered onto it for fastening. The cotton should be placed about $\frac{1}{2}$ in. in from the edges of the sills on each side and around the ends of the case slot.

Glued joints are not recommended for any part of centreboard cases because of the risk of movement previously mentioned. All surfaces should be well bedded in a mastic compound, as they used to be in white lead, with tallow added to keep it supple.

In the past the joints of centreboard case sides were frequently caulked, but this is definitely not a recommended

121

practice and is unnecessary in the cases of small craft. Fabricated steel and even bronze centreboard cases have been used but are not in keeping with a well finished small boat, though desirable in yachts.

The following sequence of fitting will ensure best results if the case is constructed as a, b, c, or d.

Bottoms of case sides bedded and placed on hog. Wood screws through keel and hog driven from below into case bottom. To ensure accurate alignment of these fastenings it is best to drill holes for them downwards through the hog and keel before the case is fitted.

Sills bedded down and screwed to sides.

Sills nailed and clenched to keel. No. 10 gauge nails at about 4 in. spacing are typical.

Headledges fastened through keel with copper clenches or bronze screws on each side, spaced to miss each other.

Care must be taken to ensure that the case or sill sides do not protrude over the slot as the centreboard will have some transverse movement and would chafe them.

Centreplates

Centreplates in general purpose dinghies are usually made of mild steel plate, cut to shape and hot-dip galvanised. For a 10 ft dinghy $\frac{3}{16}$ in. is sufficient, and $\frac{3}{8}$ in. in an 18ft boat, though if

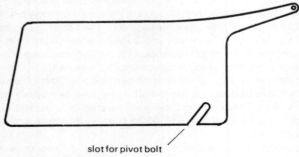

slot for pivot bolt

57   Typical centreplate shape

additional ballast is required these thicknesses often rise to $\frac{1}{4}$ in. and $\frac{1}{2}$ in., with proportional thicknesses for craft between. A common profile for plates is shown in (57), with the arm arranged to keep the shackle attaching the end of the lift clear of the top of the case when lowered. It should never be allowed to rest on the case capping as the weight of the plate will damage the timber.

Pivot bolts and fittings

The hole for the bolt on which the centreboard pivots should be a tight fit and should preferably be drilled through the sills so it can be tightened without distorting the case sides. The head and nut of the bolt should close on large metal washers about $2\frac{1}{2}$ times the bolt diameter. Rubber or neoprene washers should be fitted under these so that the wood is not crushed, and to aid watertightness of the holes; a locking nut should be fitted. It is always desirable to fit the bolt inside the boat to avoid the corrosion which occurs if fitted externally, through the keel. A galvanised steel bolt will prove strong and serviceable but bronze or stainless steel bolts are commonly used, though stainless steel can deteriorate rapidly in some salt water conditions and is expensive. If a bolt has to be fitted externally, stout washer plates should be let into the keel in way of the head and nut and the threads should be well protected against corrosion by coating with an epoxy, or with heavy paint mixed with tallow.

The fitting of a loose protective tube sleeve over the pivot bolt in way of the centreplate is a refinement but could lead to trouble if the clearance between it and the bolt becomes filled with abrasive grit or corrodes when the boat is unused.

It is good practice to fit cheek plates let into the sides of the case in way of the pivot bolt to take the compression into the case, also taking end chafe if a protective sleeve is fitted.

The centreboard should be fitted with a keep pin to secure it when almost fully up in the case and relieve strain on the hoisting arrangements. The pin should be of non-corrosive material and be fitted through the upper part of the case as far from the pivot as possible. Metal cheek plates should be sunk flush into the sides of the case and fastened by screws. These take the compression of the pin on the case sides. Sufficient travel should be left in the hoisting gear for the weight of the board to be lifted from the pin for its easy withdrawal. One end of the pin must be nosed off to enter the clearance holes in the cheek plates and the other end must have an eye for attachment to keep chain, which is attached to the case.

Cleats for halyards, centreboard lifts and sometimes sheets are often fitted to centreboard cases, but this is not good practice as cleats should be bolted to the structure, which cannot easily be done on a centreboard case, and if screwed they quickly work loose, leading to enlarged holes and probably rot. The strain on these cleats might also weaken the case by wringing and could cause leakage.

Daggerboards

A daggerboard does not need such a long keel slot as a centreboard and its case takes up less space, but the vertically sliding daggerboard is more vulnerable to damage if it strikes the ground and when partly raised in shoal water becomes an embarrassment inside the boat, getting in the way of the crew and possibly of the fore sheets. The case is made as described for a centreboard, but it is very desirable that it is connected to a thwart to take the wringing strains when, as will be inevitable, the daggerboard becomes stuck in soft mud or is forced on a lee shore due to a misjudgment in tacking. It will then be found more difficult to raise the pivoted centreboard and the turning of the boat will strain the case.

Slightly raking the daggerboard in profile will improve its resistance to damage from impact and the forward lower profile of the board should be well rounded to help it to rise when strking hard ground (58). Daggerboards may be made of steel but are usually wood, often plywood, as described for centreboards.

The case top cannot be narrowed to a slit as in a centreboard, but must be open for its full width to allow the board to slide. When the board is fully down in a short sea it sometimes lifts, particularly if made of wood. When it is partly up water can spurt up through the clearance in the slot and when removed a

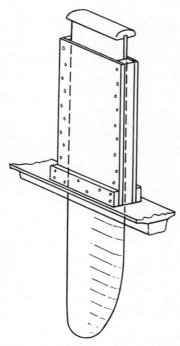

wood cover piece must be placed over the slot. The fitting of two rubber side flaps about $\frac{1}{8}$ in. thick, bedded and screw-fastened along the top of the case sides, will minimise water spurting into the boat but will make it difficult to fit the cover piece. However, if the rubbers are made to overlap in the centre they should seal the slot fairly well in most conditions and help to stop the board from jumping in a sea.

Leeboards

Leeboards are an alternative to a centreboard or daggerboard and have the advantage that the boat's interior is unobstructed by a centrecase; also the keel and hog may be of parallel

58   Typical daggerboard and case

siding and smaller dimensions, besides making building easier. The effect of a leeboard can be simply tried by hoisting a sailing dinghy's centreboard or daggerboard and holding a piece of board about $\frac{1}{2}$ in. thick by 12 in. wide by about 3 ft long over the lee side, amidships, or alternatively the blade of a broad oar. It is usually surprising how well the boat will point, but of course she will be slow in tacking. However, leeboards may be desirable in a dinghy principally used for rowing and not intended to make quick tacks. If the owner wishes for a boat for dinghy cruising the leeboards will be an advantage, enabling him to have a large unobstructed area in the boat for sleeping with an air mattress on the bottom boards.

7 Longitudinals, Thwarts and Floors

Gunwales

The gunwale, sometimes called the inwale, of a small boat is fitted around the sheer to give transverse and longitudinal strength. In good practice it should strengthen the heads of the bent timbers. There are various methods of fitting gunwales:

1 With the outer face against the inside of the sheerstrake and the lower face resting on the heads of the bent frames, which are cut away to receive it; through-fastened to the sheerstrake only. This is a traditional method but is weak if the boat has much handling in launching, etc as pulling on the gunwale is transferred to widely separated points of support at the thwart knees, breasthook and quarter knees, putting much strain on the sheerstake fastenings (59a).

2 As above but with the heads of the bent frames let or joggled into the lower face. Through-fastened to the sheerstrake only (59b).

3 With outer face against the inner faces of the bent frames and upper face flush with the sheer; through-fastened to the

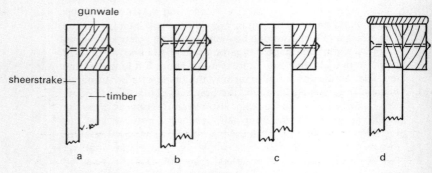

59a-d Various gunwale arrangements

heads of the bent frames and the sheerstrake. The strongest construction, which also has the advantage of allowing the boat to be stood up on her side to have dirt and stones washed out freely through the slot between the sheerstrake and the gunwale, if a capping is not fitted. Such construction usually makes the fitting of rowlock chocks easier (59c).

4 As above but with filling pieces fitted all round the sheer, between the heads of the timbers and the sheerstrake and the gunwale. These are often of softwood, glued when fitted and also fastened with a single nail clenched inside the gunwale. This method is usually finished off with a hardwood capping of the width from the outside of sheerstrake to the inside of gunwale (59d).

Gunwales are fitted after the hull is planked and timbered. Usually gunwales are tapered slightly in siding and moulding at the ends and are worked to required size well before fitting. It is then possible to put a set in them by supporting them towards each end and hanging or placing a weight in the middle to induce a curve and assist bending when fitting. In craft with much flare forward it is often necessary to cut the gunwale from a very wide board to obtain the exaggerated shape at the forward end. In normal dinghy hulls it is usually possible to bend the gunwales in one piece, but if this is considered too difficult for some reason then they may be made of two laminations, glued together with a vertical joint.

One method of setting the gunwales is to tie the ends together on the ground and force the centres apart with a strut, leaving them thus for a week or so. To fit the gunwales the moulds will have to be removed and two braces will have to be prepared to hold the sides of the boat from spreading (60). The

chocks

60   Gunwale braces

chocks on the undersides must be at least 1 in. deep, and it is best to arrange these so they can be wedged when in place to take the curve of the sides. These braces should be made to fit at one-third of the boat's length from bow and stern. Before removing the moulds the breadth at the sheerstrake should be marked on the braces.

After cleaning off the gunwales, the after brace should be removed and the gunwale placed under the forward one until its forward end butts to the aft side of the apron or stem, or into the notch which is sometimes checked out of the stem to

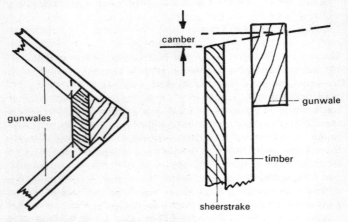

61   Gunwale notching at forward end

61a Allowing for camber when fitting gunwale

receive it (61). The aft end of the gunwale should be taken over to the opposite quarter of the boat while the forward end is cramped to the sheerstrake and/or timbers. The after end must then be cut off to allow it to lie against the transom, though not yet fitted in place. Then plenty of cramps must be worked aft along the gunwale from the stem and the after end carefully shortened further. When it is almost ready to fit home to the transom the gunwale should be fastened through the timbers and sheerstrake, starting from forward towards aft, but the extreme forward fastenings should not be driven as the breast-

128

hook fastenings will secure this. It is best to nail and clench on each alternate frame head.

As the gunwale is closed on to the timbers or sheerstrake the small excess length at the after end will usually be found to draw up, leaving a snug fit to the transom. It is well worth taking great care over this. The fastenings at the after end in way of the quarter knees must also be left out until the knees are fitted.

In fitting a gunwale it is important that the line of sheer be preserved, and that the upper face of the gunwale must be fitted slightly above the top of the sheerstrake to allow planing off to suit the sheer (61a).

If it is considered necessary, in a beamy and very full bowed dinghy, to steam the gunwales, these are best made from Canadian rock elm, in one piece and length. The steam box will not be long enough and can be extended by making a temporary extention for it from scrap wood, shipped over its end and stopped with wet sacks when the gunwales are placed inside. The forward ends should be placed in the original part of the box to obtain the best treatment. When removed they should be quickly nippered or cramped around the boat outside the sheerstrake to accept its shape before fitting. After cooling they are removed and fitted as previously described.

If it is necessary to scarph the gunwales, which is not usual in boats less than 18 ft long, the scarph should extend over at least three timbers, should be made vertically and have lips on it (43b). Gunwale scarphs are difficult to align and fit and care must be taken to ensure that the vertical faces meet all down the scarph.

A breasthook is fitted to connect the stemhead to the gunwales and the sheerstrakes, and quarter knees are necessary to connect the transom to the gunwales and sheerstrakes. These three points are those most liable to damage and sudden shock in a boat, and particular care should be taken in fitting and fastening. The breasthooks and quarter knees can be scribed and the profiles cut from the crooks or laminations (Chapter 1). The edges will have to be bevelled to suit the transom and gunwales and stem, the bevel being found by holding them in place and marking the bevels (62, 63). The breasthook should be kept slightly above the sheer to allow for

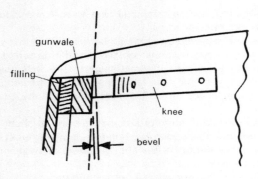

62 Bevel of quarter knees to gunwale

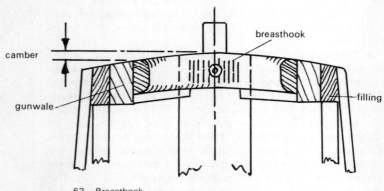

63 Breasthook

camber transversely, and quarter knees are often fitted with a slight cant to follow the top of transom. The throat of the breasthook is fastened through the stemhead and apron by a stout-gauge copper nail, clenched on the inside of the breast-hook, or by a threaded bolt set up by a nut and washer inside the breasthook.

Gunwale capping

Open boats which have the gunwale inside the heads of the bent timbers need a wood capping fitted to protect the sheer (59d). In high class work this is often of oak or Canadian rock elm, as it may be subject to wear, though English elm is best for workboats. Due to the probable breadth and thin material the capping is sometimes difficult to fit and may have to be scarphed at the round of the bow if sawn from a wide plank; alternatively it may be steamed to shape.

When the gunwale is fitted in the traditional way, above the heads of the bent timbers, it is necessary to fit rowlock cheeks or swell pieces to reinforce and give bearing in way of the rowlock plates (64). The cheeks should be of hardwood at least 9 in. long and if possible should be fastened across two bent frames. However, as the relation of a rowlock to a thwart is fixed, this may not be possible. A filling piece must be fitted

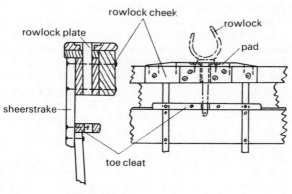

64   Rowlock cheek and toe cleat

131

between the gunwale and the sheerstrake, all through-fastened together with the rowlock cheek.

After the rowlock stem hole is bored it should be burned out with a red hot iron to prevent the wood fibres swelling when wet. The rowlock plate is often sunk into the capping but is better sunk into a thin hardwood pad, about the same thickness as the capping and extending the length of the cheek, but bevelled down at the ends. This can be glued and screwed to the capping. It raises the rowlock clear of the sheer capping and avoids wear on it by the oars. These pads should be about 10 in. long by the combined width of the sheerstrake, timbers and gunwale, and not less than $\frac{1}{2}$ in. thick. Holly is the best wood for them, but oak, elm or beech are suitable.

When boring the rowlock hole the bit should be kept parallel with the planking so the stem of the rowlock will be clear of it when dropped into place. The rowlock plate can be fitted by putting the rowlock in the hole with the plate on it and scribing around the plate. If possible the rowlock hole should be kept within the filling, leaving the gunwale intact. When driving the fastenings for the cheek piece these should be kept clear of the rowlock hole.

The lower end of the rowlock stem must fit into a toe cleat a suitable distance below the gunwale, to suit the stem. The length of the toe cleat must be sufficient to get two clenched nails on either side of the hole. The cleat must be held in place and marked for position of the hole from the stem, bored and then fastened. It is best to fit it on a plank land. The thickness of toe cleats varies from $\frac{1}{2}$ in. to $\frac{3}{8}$ in., and of the cheek pieces about $\frac{3}{4}$ in.

Rowlock position is related to the freeboard of the boat and the height of the thwart on which the rower sits. A usual position in a dinghy is 11 in. aft of the after edge of a thwart. In larger boats, particularly those using long oars, and workboats, the rowlocks are fitted up to 14 in. aft of a thwart.

Traditional boats are often fitted with thole pins instead of rowlocks (65). These are still in common use at West Mersea, Essex, and in other places. Tholes are best made from holly or oak and the gunwale pads become more important in taking the direct chafe of the leathered oar looms working on them, protecting the gunwale, and the thickness should be increased to $\frac{3}{4}$ in.

132

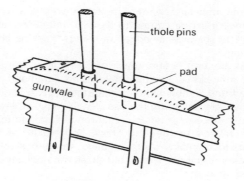

65   Thole pins

Rowlocks are sold in pairs with two rowlock plates. They are made of malleable iron (galvanised), gunmetal, or sometimes bronze or reinforced nylon. Of all these galvanised iron rowlocks are the most reliable at those crucial times when great strain may be put on the rowlocks by hard rowing in a seaway or an emergency. The other materials have been known to break under sudden strain, but of course do not rust and look more yachty. Rowlocks are generally supplied in sizes, measured between the horns, of 2 in. to 3 in., rising in quarter inches.

Leather oar strips were used instead of thole pins or rowlocks in some American small boats.

Risings

These are light side stringers which support the thwarts as well as the bent timbers. They are invariably of much lighter scantlings than the gunwales and are fastened through the bent timbers and planking (69). The risings will not follow the sheer but should support the thwarts at an even height above the hog. Care must be taken to fit them at equal heights on both sides of the boat as otherwise the thwarts may fit badly and require letting into the tops of the risings to seat properly. Risings need not be carried to the stem and are usually stopped

133

two or three timbers forward of the fore thwart. If a stern bench is fitted they must be carried to the last timber forward of the transom. The sharp inner edges of risings must be chamfered before fitting.

In heavy boats it is often desirable to fit two side stringers; the upper may act as a rising if thwarts are fitted and the lower should be fitted just below the turn of the bilge. A bilge stringer should never be fitted into the curve of the bilge where this is a small or tight radius, as where it is through-fastened to the bent frames it will cause them to crack, and make the structure inefficient. In a heavy craft the bilge stringer usually has a breasthook and quarter knees, but these are unnecessary in an ordinary small boat.

Thwarts and stern benches

The position of thwarts should be carefully considered in relation to a boat's rig and in any boat intended for serious rowing. Their height depends on the freeboard and length of oar to be used. In a small boat of average freeboard the amidship thwart should not be more than 6 in. below the rowlock for comfortable rowing and the forward thwart not less then 6 in. due to the constricted spread of the forward rowlocks. The least height above the bottom boards at which an average person can sit comfortably is 9 in., but this is too high for comfortable pulling; in attempting to improve rowing capabilities it may be desirable to block up the foot stretchers a few inches above the bottom boards.

In pleasure dinghies and yachts' boats, thwarts and stern benches are usually of Honduras mahogany, teak, iroko, or one of the varieties of African mahogany. In working boats they are often of oak, elm, red pine or larch. An average width for a thwart is 7 in.

With the height and position of thwarts determined, their length is measured by pinch rods, or two light battens overlapped and cramped together to obtain the true length at the forward and aft edges of a thwart (66). When the battens are adjusted a pencil mark is made across one of them and against the end of the other; the battens are uncramped, and when

134

reset on the plank from which the thwart is to be cut will give an accurate dimension.

The lengths of the thwart edges should be divided and the centreline of the boat marked. The thwart ends are fitted and bevelled to the planking and timbers. If the thwart jams before it seats properly on the risings it is probably binding on a timber which may be bearing away from the planking where it crosses a land. The undercutting necessary is usually more than one

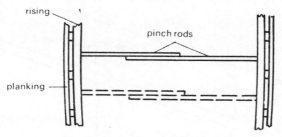

66   Pinch rods to measure length of thwarts

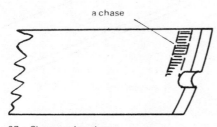

67   Chase cut in a thwart

would expect. Thwarts should seat well on the risings without movement. If they are uneven it is necessary to cut a chase in the thwart to seat it properly (67). The ends are, of course, cut and fitted around the timbers.

A thwart more than 5 ft long should be supported by a stanchion under its centre, down to the hog. These thwart stanchions may be plain, straight-grained timber or, as in the elegant yachts' and ships boats of the past, an ornamental turned support. These are usually fitted with the thwart and the ends of the stanchion are square. The upper ships into a square hole in a square hardwood chock, about $\frac{3}{4}$ in. thick, which is glued and screwed to the underside of the thwart. The lower end is usually tenoned to fit in a mortice cut in the top of the hog (68). These posts save more than their weight as thwarts can be reduced in thickness where the span is halved.

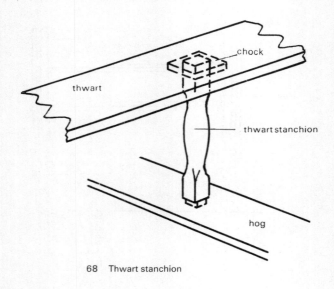

68   Thwart stanchion

The stern thwart or stern bench will also be seated on the risings and must also be supported by a wooden horizontal bearer screwed and bedded to the transom on either side of the sternpost, with its upper edge level with the tops of the risings.

If side benches are fitted, as they always were in ships' and yachts' boats, though they are now uncommon, they should be checked into the stern bench and the after thwart at the ends, and possibly further supported by butt pieces underneath, screw-fastened and glued to the thwarts and benches.

136

Knees

To tie the sides of a boat firmly together, the ends of the thwarts are connected to the gunwales and upper side planking by vertical knees, usually fitted in pairs at the forward and after edges of amidship thwarts and singly on the forward thwart, depending on the type and size of boat (69). The knees will all be of similar size and shape, and time and labour will be saved by selecting an elbow shaped piece of grown timber to be sawn into a number of knees of the required thickness at once. Oak is the common wood for knees but will shrink considerably unless very well seasoned, and even then will contract slightly when

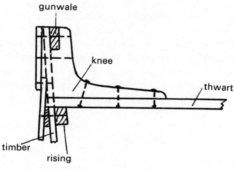

69   Thwart knee

cut. Crooks from the branches of apple trees were commonly used in England and America. Although hard to work they are tough and durable. Ash was sometimes used in England, and horse chestnut, but both are prone to rot. Other alternatives are English elm and, in the USA, hackmatack; either parts of branches or roots, providing they are well seasoned. Laminated knees are described in Chapter 1.

If double knees are fitted to a thwart they are best finished about $\frac{5}{8}$ in. thick, so the knees must be cut $\frac{3}{4}$ in. to allow for planing. If single knees are fitted they should be about 1 in. thick off the saw. The toe of the arm on the thwart may be tapered down in profile to about $\frac{3}{16}$ in., but the heads must

137

always be deep or they will crack at the gunwale fastening.

Traditionally the heads of all knees are let into the gunwale about $\frac{1}{4}$ in. To avoid splitting they should be left about 1 in. above the gunwale until bored and fastened by a copper nail driven from the outside through the sheerstrake, gunwale and head of the knee, on the inside of which the nail is rooved and clenched. The vertical arm of a knee usually has two other clenched fastenings through the plank lands, clenched inside the knee. The arm of the knee on the thwart is usually fastened to it by either three copper nails clenched under the thwart, or by three bronze screws which are flushed off underneath by hacksaw and file, after being driven. Knees must be well bedded when finally fitted. The knee must first have the lower arm trued for fitting to the upper face of the thwart.

They may be marked from a plywood or pine board template carefully fitted to the upper surface of the thwart, the inside face of hull planking, and around the gunwale. Alternatively the knee itself can be prepared and fitted. In either case the marking may be carried out as shown in (70). A pair of screw dividers are opened slightly wider than the greatest gap between the boat's sheerstrake and the template or perhaps the

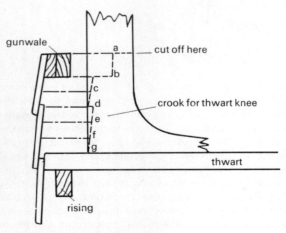

70   Marking out a thwart knee

knee itself. A mark is made at a and repeated at b, c, d, e, f and g, being careful to hold the dividers exactly parallel and horizontal for accurate marking. The resulting spots outline the profile of the knee, and if carefully cut and planed it should fit properly. However, it will also need to be side-bevelled to the curve of planking and gunwale so that the other side of the knee also fits to the planking and gunwale. This can be marked as described.

Instead of dividers boatbuilders often use a parallel ended, narrow wood block, or dummy. Its width is the greatest gap as described for the dividers method, and a sharp pencil is held firmly at its end as it is run around the profile to be marked. The dummy should be narrow, as when going round a curve only one edge of it should touch, to ensure accuracy.

In working boats and yachts' hack boats, the sides are further strengthened for bumping alongside larger vessels by fitting horizontal knees (lodging knees) in numbers and positions depending on the intended service. One at each end of a thwart is sufficient for a hack boat, but workboats likely to be abused, ie trawlers' boats, dredger boats and mooring boats, etc will need them doubled. The longitudinal arms of these knees are fastened to the planking by copper nails rooved and clenched inside the knee. The athwartships arm should be let into the edge of the thwart about $\frac{1}{4}$ in. If, as is possible in a working boat, the thwart is of pine, the arm should be fastened by three large bronze screws.

Floors

If these are required in the boat's structure they are fitted after planking and timbering is completed and the gunwales and risings are fitted. If the boat has a centreboard this will also have been fitted.

Floors are unnecessary in a small pulling dinghy, but are usually fitted in sailing boats and larger pulling boats such as gigs, where the bottom at the ends rises and the bent timbers cannot be continuous across the boat. The floors provide the required continuity of transverse strength. Where necessary they should be sided about 1 in. and carried as far up the bilge as the level of the bottom boards permit. If the upper faces of floors are to act as bearers for bottom boards they may be excessively deep for the strength required. The siding should not be less then $3\frac{1}{2}$ times the diameter of the largest fastening to be driven through them. If possible, floor depths on the centreline should not be less then 3 times the floor siding, tapering to about $1\frac{1}{2}$ times the siding at ends. In long boats floors are often spaced about 4 ft apart and it has always been traditional practice to fit floors alongside a timber or frame. However, this is questionable as the abutting faces are afterwards never painted, and it is preferable to fit floors about $1\frac{1}{4}$ in. away from the side of timbers.

Floors are particularly necessary in working boats which may be left, loaded, to settle on a hard. They must also be fitted adjacent to the mast steps in sailing boats. Straight floors may be of oak, iroko, teak or hackmatack, and shaped floors of oak, larch or hackmatack. If the bottom has much shape the floors should be cut from timber with similar grain shape or alternatively may be laminated with horizontal, glued laminations, which will probably be stronger, though more time-consuming to make.

Particular care must be taken in fitting floors in way of a centreboard case, where at least one pair should be in the form of a knee, either grown or laminated. See centreboard case construction, Chapter 6.

Floors are cut approximately to shape from a template lifted from position in the boat, and are planed to siding on both sides. They must be about $\frac{1}{2}$ in. deeper than when finished to allow for fitting. The floors are set in the boat between nails lightly tacked in on each side to keep them upright. A rule or

marking for finished floor shape

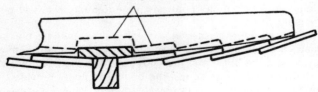

71   Marking a floor

small, parallel sided block is used to make a pencil mark of the accurate profile of the inner face of the hog and planking on each side of the floor, thus also producing the bevel. Limber holes must be marked at each plank land and at the junction of hog and garboard, for adequate drainage (71).

The floor is removed and about four saw cuts are made across it from the lower edge down to the pencil lines representing each plank face, and those parts are then worked away with a chisel. The floor is again tried between the nails and any adjustments marked on it. Before it is finally fitted the limbers are carefully cut away.

Holes are bored from inside the planking for the floor fastenings, guided by a line marked across the planking to represent the centre of floor. The throat is bored for the throat fastening and the face is well luted with a mastic or lead bedding before fitting and fastening.

Floors may be through-fastened to the hog and keel in large boats, or bronze or galvanised screw-fastened to the hog and keel in small ones. The arms may be bronze or galvanised screw-fastened from outside the hull planking, but the toes of

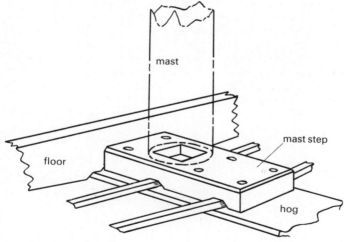

72 Typical mast step

floors should be through-fastened with copper clenches. Good fitting of floors to planking and hog is essential and they should be well bedded on a mastic compound or red and white lead paint.

When masts are stepped on the hog or keel in small boats the heel of a wood mast should shoulder down from round to square section, with a depth of about 2 in., which fits into a hardwood chock about 3 in. deep. This is notched over at least two timbers and accurately fitted to the top of hog or keel, to which it is fastened by at least four bronze screws. A floor must be fitted near the mast step to distribute forces from the mast heel (72).

8 Deck Beams and Decks

Deck beams

If possible both the temporary braces should be kept on the sheer until the thwarts and deck beams are fitted. If a brace has to be removed it forms a template when put back, which will maintain the boat's correct beam.

Deck beams are cambered and the usual amount of camber, sometimes called crop or round of beam, will be about $\frac{1}{2}$ in. per foot of beam in small boats, taken at the greatest beam. It is best to set out a beam mould as in (73), L equalling the length of beam at the greatest breadth of the boat. If this is 5 ft, then we will need a camber of 5 $\times$ $\frac{1}{2}$ in., which is $2\frac{1}{2}$ in. With a pair of compasses a semicircle is drawn at the centre of the mould

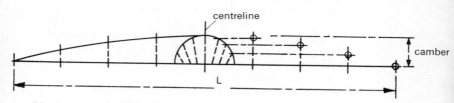

73   Setting out beam camber mould

and each half of the semicircle is divided into an equal number of parts; at least four. The half breadth on each side of the centreline is also divided into the same number of spaces, and lines projected vertically and horizontally from these spots will intersect and provide points through which a batten can be bent to give a fair line of camber. Each beam in the boat will usually be a different length and all dimensions for working them must be taken about the centreline of the boat.

The greatest span beam is fitted first, care being taken to see that it is at the correct height on its upper side at the centre, as it will regulate all the other beams. In a small boat beams forward of this may be fitted to a height at centreline obtained by stretching a taut line from the upper side of this beam to a position on the centreline of the back of apron or stem, at a height of the underside of the deck. This should be carefully kept taut.

In small halfdecked boats the undersides of the beams are rarely seen and may be cut straight instead of cambered, unless weight saving is desired. They are also stiffer if thus fitted, and beams in way of the mast, which will have a mast partner chock between them, will need the additional depth.

Besides bearing the deck the beams act as transverse ties to the sides of the boat, and their end connections to the gunwale, or shelf, as it becomes known when fitted to take beam ends, must be designed to resist the outwards spreading of the boat's sheer. Various methods of beam end construction are shown in (74a–d).

a. A method once commonly used in sailing dinghy construction. The beam end is bevelled to follow the half breadth curve and the shelf is checked out to receive it. It is fastened with a nail driven through the shelf and into the beam from one side, on the skew.

b. A common method in yacht building, the half dovetail, resisting pull. It is difficult to fit well as it has a blind end and in small beams the dovetail is shallow.

c. The above remarks apply.

d. The best connection. The half dovetail is carried through the width of the shelf making it easier to work, provided the shelf is made adequately deep to accept the dovetails and allow a housing to be cut in the shelf's inner face, horizontally, to bear the lower face of the beam end, before the dovetail. Besides relieving the weight on the dovetail the housing also allows some transverse shrinkage of the beam ends without ugly and inefficient gaps appearing at the shelf; particularly likely with oak beams.

Beams are traditionally of hardwoods such as oak, but with the scarcity of seasoned oak, woods such as iroko are being used in quite large craft. Laminated spruce beams are probably the best now obtainable, being light, strong and of course made

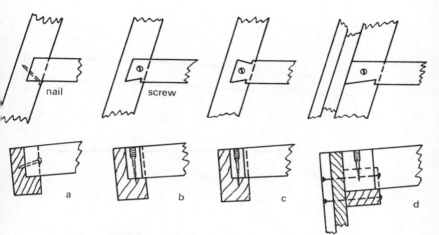

74a-d Various arrangements of beam end construction

to a mould of the correct camber which reduces the labour of shaping. Pine and spruce are often used for beams in sailing dinghies.

If softwood beams are fitted it is best to construct the beam ends as (74a). If part dovetailed they will have little strength and will tend to split at the shoulder of the dovetail, but if carried full depth the strength of the beam is retained. Housing in the beam end remains practical and desirable.

Setting out beam end joints requires careful thought as the gunwale or shelf is usually not vertical but raked outwards, and the sheer further confuses clear appreciation of the approach. The method of setting out a dovetail is shown in (75). The beam is cut to length with a little to spare at each end. The dovetail is marked off and cut on the beam first; then the mortice for it is marked off on the shelf, from the beam, and cut. The beam is laid in position and a mark made on the shelf so that, when cut, it will fit back in the same place. A rule or straightedge is held plumb, if necessary with a spirit level held by a helper, to produce the spots A-a, B-b, C-c and draw line B-C, which is the sawing line for the face of the shelf. Draw A-d parallel as the line to which the beam end will be sawed off on both the aft and forward faces of the beam. On B-B mark B-e at one-third

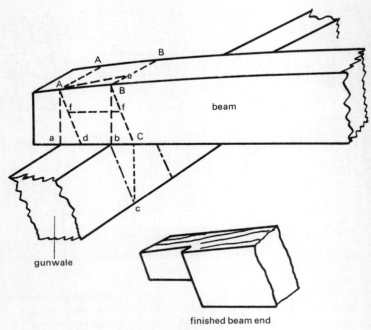

beam

gunwale

finished beam end

75 Setting out beam end dovetail

the siding of the beam and draw the dovetail line A-e. Saw out
the dovetail on the lines marked and then mark off the line f-f at
one-third the depth of the beam, then cut away the wood below
it. Set out the mortice on the marks already made and cut
inside the lines to ensure a good fit, as little more can always be
eased away but sound wood can never be added in such a joint.
If the dovetail is a bad fit, the amateur may try to improve it by
wedging with a chip of wood on the plain face of the beam,
securing it with glue and a skew nail.

The beam ends and shelf may be tried to ensure accurate
camber by making an external round of beam mould, scribed off
the beam mould proper, which can be applied as they are
trimmed down.

Typical beam arrangements for the deck of a small sailing
boat with an open cockpit are shown by (76). Lodging knees

146

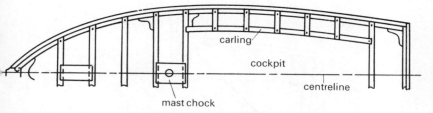

carling

cockpit

centreline

mast chock

76 Typical beam arrangement for a small sailing boat

are unnecessary in small boats with plywood decks. They are
fitted to mast beams in traditionally laid decks to distribute
mast forces into the hull.

The sides of cockpits and hatches must be bounded by
carlings (or carlines), to preserve strength in the deck framing
and provide grounds for coamings. The beam ends are usually
housed or dovetailed into the carlings and these must be
deeper than the beams and have adequate siding for the beam
end connections. Carlings must be fitted with the inner face
vertical, which is difficult due to the carling following the curve
of deck sheer and the usually curved plan shape of the cockpit.
In a short cockpit, carlings will be amply stiff, but in a long one
they may need some support, which is best achieved by light
struts (77) which can also act as stowages for oars and
boathook. Alternatively the traditional knees can be fitted, but
these are much heavier.

In small boats the coamings are usually screwed to the inner
face of the carlings and the after beam. If it is desired to have a
curved front or after end to the coaming, the curve will have to
be chocked out from the face of the carlings and the beam. If
square corners are intended. a rebated corner post should be
fitted using one of the methods indicated in (78). If the
coamings are run forward to a point on the foredeck the joint
should be made on a chock (79). Any corners of coamings
should be strengthened by a small knee (80) as they will
certainly be climbed over or pulled at various times. It is usual
to fit a hardwood beading around and over the joint between a
plywood or canvas covered deck and the coamings, as in small
boats this joint cannot be caulked.

When a mast is stepped through the deck a substantial chock

147

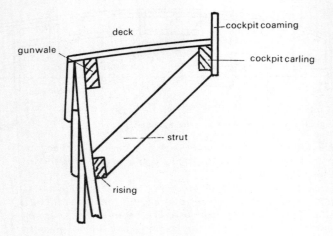

77 Cockpit carling support strut

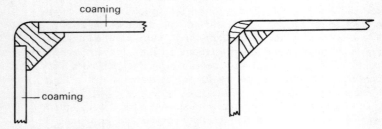

78 Cockpit coaming corner posts

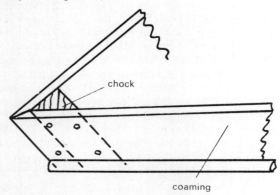

79 Cockpit coaming forward chock

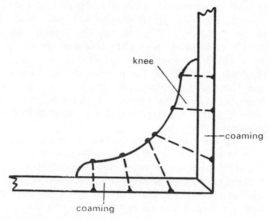

80   Cockpit coaming knee

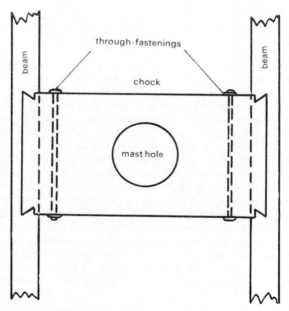

81   Mast partner chock

must be fitted on the centreline between the mast beams. In small craft the chock is often of mahogany, oak or pine if the boat is built lightly. Its thickness will vary from $\frac{3}{4}$ in. in a 12-footer to $1\frac{1}{2}$ in. in a 20-footer. The chock's upper surface must be flush with the tops of beams and cambered to suit the round of beam. The ends are dovetailed and housed into the faces of the beams (81). The partner chock is always laid with the grain of the timber longitudinally and may be strengthened by fitting two clenches through it, transversely (81). Lodging the chock $\frac{1}{2}$ in. into the beams will hold better than many longitudinal fastenings.

The mast hole is cut in it after fitting. If a circular rubber mast collar is fitted the hole may be made with an expanding bit. If the mast is wedged at deck, now uncommon in such small craft, the hole is made with six or eight sides to give bearing for the hardwood wedges. Alternatively, the mast hole may be cut by boring a ring of holes around the marked out circumference and cutting away the wood between them, finishing off with a rasp.

Deck

Before laying a deck it is best to paint or varnish anything below it which will afterwards be difficult to reach.

Marine grade plywood is the best material for decks of small boats. The plywood generally used in Britain is to BSS 1088, but the Dutch-made Bruynzeel plywood is excellent material in the author's experience. Plywood is usually supplied in sheets 8 ft by 4 ft and it is often necessary to scarph these when laying a deck. This may be done by butting them on a beam if the panels are laid transversely, but unless the deck is to be covered by a fabric, such a butt is liable to hold water which will be absorbed into the edges of the plywood causing eventual delamination. Alternatively, the panels may be butted longitudinally on a centreline butt strap let flush into the tops of the deck beams (82). However, this weakens the beams, which must be made deeper to compensate. The best method of joining is to scarph and glue the panels together, making a scarph width six times the thickness of the plywood. This may be temporarily secured

150

by small screws which become superfluous when the glue has set. The plywood may be fastened to the beams with bronze ringed nails or with galvanised steel nails, though the heads of these will eventually rust. It is unnecessary to fasten the decks of small boats to beams with screws.

In a painted plywood deck the nails should be punched under-flush and their heads stopped over with a hard-setting compound. If the plywood deck is to be covered with the traditional painted canvas or a nylon cloth coated with a resin, then the fastenings may be galvanised steel nails.

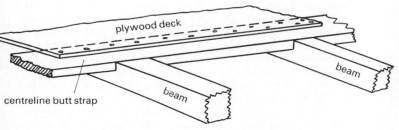

82   Butt strap for plywood deck

Many builders favour gluing the deck to the deck beams, but consider this of very doubtful value as it is very difficult to ensure a gluing fit on all surfaces if a panel is being fitted to them. It is preferable to bed the deck on mastic, which ensures the watertightness of the bond and gives a slight tolerance.

The edges of plywood decks must be very well protected. If there is not to be a fabric covering edges should be sealed with an epoxy coating and covered by a capping piece which may also be a rubbing strake, well fitted and bedded in a waterproof mastic. Edges must be nailed to the gunwale, and if the timbers are large and the sheerstrake thick, may also be screw-fastened to the sheerstrake to ensure watertightness at the sheer. Any other edges of the plywood at cockpit, hatch or mast openings must also be sealed.

Plywood up to 10 mm thick may be bent over an average camber without trouble, but when this thickness is exceeded on small boats it may be better to consider fitting two skins of

151

equal thickness and gluing them together. The difference in time taken may be little.

Despite the superiority of plywood decks some owners still prefer to lay a deck of tongued and grooved boards covered with painted canvas. T and G is not so easily obtained as formerly, when it was commonly used in house building. A minimum thickness of $\frac{1}{2}$ in. will probably have to be used, which will mean a deck of acceptable weight only for hulls over about 16 ft length.

The tongued and grooved boards are fitted longitudinally, and as a covering board is unnecessary, because they are to be covered with canvas, the ends are run out over the sheer and cut off flush with the edge of the sheerstrake. Narrow widths of about 4 in. are better than wide planks, and they should be merely pushed together, hand-tight, not cramped up hard, to avoid undue swelling and movement of the deck when well wetted. Fastenings may be galvanised nails or ringed nails. The heads must be punched under-flush and be stopped over with putty or a hard-setting compound.

After planking the deck is planed smooth and fair and given a generous coat of thick lead paint. When this is almost dry a second thick coat is added and the canvas may be laid. There are two schools of thought on the best method; one holds that the canvas should be seamed on a sailmaker's sewing machine and soaked in fresh water before fitting. The other maintains that it must be fitted dry to absorb the paint, and that the seams must be doubled over and fastened to the deck with a double row of tacks. I believe in the latter, the canvas being strained down smooth and secured with $\frac{3}{8}$ in. tacks.

The usual weight of canvas for covering decks is 8 or 10 oz. In a boat with a transom, stretch the canvas across the stern as tightly as possible and fasten it with copper tacks across the stern and for about 2 ft forward of the transom. Then gather the canvas in forward, or roll it up around a pole and clamp it securely to it with several cramps. Put a tackle on the pole ends and heave it as tight as possible, longitudinally, or alternatively get about six people to heave on it as hard as possible. The canvas is then pulled transversely and tacked to the edge of the deck with $\frac{5}{8}$ in. or $\frac{3}{4}$ in. copper tacks. When the whole deck is covered its edges are protected by rectangular or half-round hardwood chafing pieces, screw-fastened to the deck edge and the sheerstrake, over the canvas. These must be well bedded. Afterwards the excess canvas below the lower edge of the chafing pieces is trimmed away with a sharp knife.

It is difficult to get paint to spread on canvas and the first coat on after fitting should be of thinned flat paint. When this is dry a further two coats should be given. Beware of painting the canvas with gloss paint as this will harden and crack; many coats of flat paint will give it longer life. If desired the seams could be covered with hardwood protective pieces, though unless these were on the centreline they would be unsightly.

Sometimes owners particularly desire a traditionally laid deck with caulked seams and there are two methods of constructing this:

With seams parallel to the centreline and the plank ends nibbed into a covering board.

With seams swept with the curve of the half breadth at sheer and the plank ends nibbed into a kingplank on the centreline.

The first is the most common method in small boats and the centreplank is usually made wide enough to carry the mast hole and, perhaps, a mooring bitt. Sometimes the kingplank is of teak or Honduras mahogany, bright varnished, and on some boats the covering boards are also varnished, the remainder of the deck often being scrubbed pine. In choosing a deck of this type an owner should remember it is heavy, costly and may eventually leak.

The covering board will need to be sawn out in segments which are scarphed together. It will land on the beam shelf, which must be fitted slightly above the sheerline to allow for bevelling to the beam camber. To withstand the strain of caulking, the covering boards must be well fastened to the shelf and the sheerstrake with bronze screws. Where the side covering boards meet the covering board which is fitted across the transom, the joint is mitred. At the forward end the side covering boards are butted to the sides of the kingplank. All these joints are caulked as for the planking.

Covering boards should be cut from long, wide planks to reduce the number of joints, which should be made with hook

153

scarphs as considerable strain can be imposed on them at times. In light construction the covering boards are often made thicker than usual and are rebated down into the tops of the beam ends. The inner edge of the covering board is then rebated out to take the nibbed ends of the deck planking. More usually the nibbed ends of the deck planks, where they are clear of the beam shelf, are supported by hardwood chocks fitted under the planking between the deck beams.

Deck planking is laid with the grain uppermost (83), and the seams are prepared by tapering the plank edges (83), which lie close together at the bottom but are mouthed at the top to receive the caulking and stopping. Planking of a laid deck is

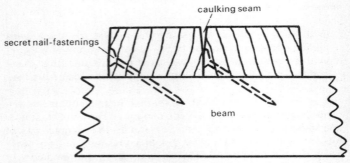

83   Laid deck planking, seams for caulking, and secret nailing to beams

usually secret-nailed to the beams (83), which avoids fastenings showing on the surface. Brass cut nails are traditionally used, but galvanised will last as long. In larger craft the swept deck planking is usually also side-fastened with brass dowels, half driven into a plank which has been laid, leaving the other half protruding, on which the next plank is driven sideways, when it is fitted. These dowels secure the planks against the tendency to spring upward resulting from the curve.

Before caulking the seams are painted with thick lead paint which is left to dry. Such a deck has to be caulked with either oakum or boat cotton. In the size of boats we are considering, boat cotton is usual. The strands of cotton are purchased in balls and before use several strands are spun into a loose string,

154

usually three strands for decks of small craft, depending on the width of seam. This is done by bending a nail and placing it in a hand or electric drill chuck and slowly spinning the rope thus formed. This is then ready to drive in the seams, which have to be made of even width with a making iron, a blunt form of caulking iron. The cotton is then lightly driven into the seam with a caulking iron of finer blade. Caulking a seam with cotton or oakum is best learned by observing a professional boatbuilder. The principal action to note is that the caulking is first gathered along the seam in loops or bights with the caulking iron before it is driven into the seam to fill it evenly and firmly. The iron is lubricated during caulking by occasionally dipping it into a small box or tin of cotton waste or teased-out oakum soaked in linseed oil. This keeps it free in the seam and allows it to drive more easily.

It is not possible to give concrete directions as to how hard the cotton should be driven as it depends on the width of seam, type of wood and cotton and the skill of the caulker. If in doubt get a professional to do it. Too hard blows will force the caulking right through the seam, force the planks apart and spoil the seam.

After caulking, the seams are gone over carefully with an iron to harden them down and they are ready to be payed. Traditionally this is done with 'glue', a patent derivative of pitch which is bought in blocks in tins, broken out and heated in a 'glue kettle'. An iron pot is heated over a fire or flame burner and in this the glue is brought to a hot, liquid state, ready to be poured into the seams. This is done with a glue ladle, which is run along the seams leaving the seam filled with solidifying glue and as much excess on the deck surface, to be scraped off after it has cooled. Any large, heavy gauge pot will do for a kettle and a large spoon or kitchen pouring ladle will do to pour the glue.

Traditionally, ordinary pitch was used for paying and this was heated in the same way, but tallow was added, gradually, to give it some flexibility. Pitch and tallow can be tried before use by dropping a little in water and testing the resultant lump. If it is brittle there is too little tallow. The glue was devised to have some suppleness so that when the deck planking shrank or swelled, the paying in the seam did not crack and let water penetrate to the caulking.

155

9 Finishing the Hull

Rubbing strakes

Dinghy rubbing strakes should be of hardwood, preferably of Canadian rock elm. They are usually fitted under the land of the sheerstrake, which provides a fair sweep location and assists in resisting upward pressures such as when alongside quays, etc. If fitted in this way the top of the rubbing strake must be flat to bear against the plank land.

Rubbing strakes are often of the sections shown in (84). They are best through-fastened to the planking and the timbers, but in some regions are screw-fastened. For boats up to about 14 ft long the rubbing strake can be worked from timber $\frac{3}{4} \times 1$ in., from 14 to 20 ft from timber $1\frac{1}{8} \times 1\frac{1}{4}$ in. to $1\frac{1}{4} \times 1\frac{3}{4}$ in. Forward, the rubber is carried out to the side of the stem, being bevelled off as necessary. Aft, it finishes on the transom; in working boats with a badge piece as shown (85). This acts as a quarter fender.

In open rowing boats it is usual to fit whiskers (86) made from oak about $\frac{1}{2}$ in. thick, to take the chafe of the painter or mooring rope. These are usually through-fastened to the sheerstrake and gunwale, but are screwed to the stem, which they also support.

Bilge keels

The size and position of bilge keels will depend on the shape of the boat and the conditions of use. As they slow a boat they should be as small as possible, consistent with their function of protecting the lower strakes from chafe on the ground. If a boat is intended to ground regularly on a hard, stony bottom it is desirable to make them deep enough to give protection.

In a small boat they may be of English elm, oak or Canadian rock elm, about $\frac{5}{8} \times \frac{3}{4}$ in. section, tapered forward and aft and

156

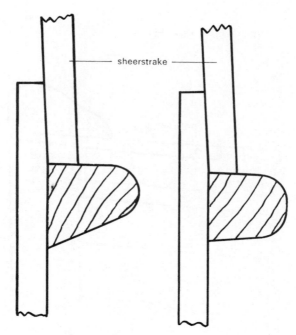

84   Rubbing strake shapes

85   Quarter-badge pieces

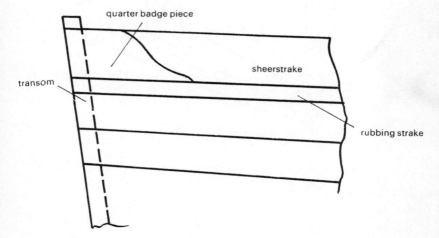

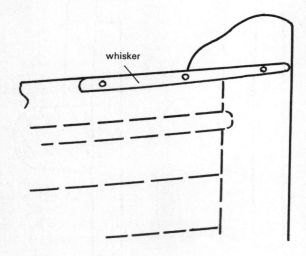

whisker

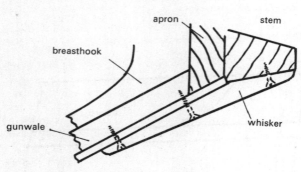

apron

stem

breasthook

gunwale

whisker

86 Bow whiskers

fastened on the land of a plank where the keel will take the boat's weight without the bottom planking touching the ground when the boat is on a reasonably level surface. In a 20 ft boat the bilge keels might be worked from $1\frac{1}{2} \times 1\frac{1}{2}$ in. wood. They should be through-fastened through the planking and timbers with copper nails clenched on rooves.

Bilge keels which are fitted to larger hulls to reduce rolling sometimes sustain considerable force, afloat and grounded, and strong through-fastenings should be fitted. If at all possible, the ends of at least some of the floors should be extended up the bilge to support these keels and fastenings. Deep bilge keels will need to be cut to profile shape from a template lifted from the boat.

Bottom boards

These were traditionally known as burden boards, carrying the boat's load of goods or personnel. The construction of these vital items seldom receives proper attention. They should never be varnished, always of scrubbed finish. English elm is the most suitable timber, but clear-grained pine, white cedar or Port Orford cedar are also used. Teak is unsuitable as it splits easily at the edges of the boards and can be very dangerous as its splinters may cause septic wounds.

Typical scantlings vary from $\frac{5}{16}$ in. thickness in a 10 ft dinghy to $\frac{3}{8}$ in. in an 18-footer. Bottom boards are rarely made as a continuous, close-seamed floor, which is favoured in working boats, but usually as open (longitudinally slatted) boards which are transversely strapped together with timber of the same thickness. In a dinghy without a centreboard case the bottom boards are made in two main parts, one on each side of a centreline single board which has two slots towards its ends, which slip over staples driven into the hog. This centre board is held down firmly by wedge-shaped wooden pegs which slip through the staples. The slatted side pieces probably have three transverse straps on each side and the inner ends of these slip under the edges of the centre board to keep them in place. The outer edges of the boards fit up to a bilge rising and are secured by wooden turnbuttons which pivot on a bronze screw driven into the rising fitted with its lower inner edge parallel to the bottom board edge. The object is to have boards which are easily removable for cleaning, painting or repair, but which will be firmly fixed when the boat is in use.

Rowing stretchers

Modern dinghies do not often have stretchers, but these should be fitted in some form as it is much easier to row properly with bracing for the feet. Stretchers are best formed by screwing and gluing transverse strips to the bottom boards, carefully positioned to suit the rower's feet. These are much better than the traditional stretchers which fitted in wood racks for adjustment to suit leg length but cluttered the boat's bottom.

One variation is to cut a series of spaced triangular holes in a wide centre bottom board at suitable positions aft of the rowing thwarts, to provide bracing for the feet. However, these are usually too close together to be effective and can be dangerous if a heel is caught in them. The corners of these cutouts must be well rounded to avoid splitting the wood. The centreboard must be arranged well above the boat's bottom so the rower's heels do not touch the boat's structure.

Rowing seats

Some rowing enthusiasts have advocated rowing seats instead of thwarts. These are wooden stools with a wooden top shaped to give comfortable seating. The flat sides of the stool have straight bottoms fitting inside wooden longitudinal strips which are screwed to the bottom boards and act as guides, retaining the stool in a correct transverse position but allowing it to be moved longitudinally to suit the rower's position relative to the rowlocks. Sometimes the sides of the seat are cut away from the bottom, about 3 in. in from the corners, and arch up in a shallow curve. This allows the rower to slip his heels under the cutouts and steady his stroke, though this must be more tiring than using a stretcher.

160

Rudders

There are two principal types of small boat rudder; fixed blade and lifting blade. The fixed blade is a traditional form for pulling and sailing craft where the blade need not extend below the bottom of the keel. Many sailing dinghies were fitted with fixed blade rudders which extended well below the keel but these are a nuisance in shoal water, when they may become unshipped on striking the ground and are awkward to stow in the boat when not in use. Basically they are made from three parts; the mainpiece, which may be fabricated from one or two pieces of wood, and the two side cheeks which reinforce the rudder head against the twisting strains of the tiller. The cheeks are carried down to about the waterline and are through-fastened to the mainpiece with copper clenches.

Even if a single wide board is available from which to cut a rudder (or a centreboard) it is better to make it of two boards as a precaution against warping. The wood should be rift sawn, that is with the grain of the annular rings at right angles to the widest surface. When the two parts are joined, edge to edge, they should be planed so that the grain in one runs opposite to the grain in the other. If warping then occurs, the distortion in one part will offset the distortion in the other instead of aggravating it, which happens when two boards are joined with the grains running in the same direction.

The profile of the forward edge of a fixed sailing rudder should be well rounded to assist it to lift and ride over an obstacle. The forward and after edges should be well rounded or shaped in section to improve sailing efficiency.

The lifting type of rudder has been used for at least 80 years, and probably much longer. Construction is similar to the fixed rudder except that the mainpiece stops short of the bottom of the cheeks, which are heavier than in the fixed type and carry a pivot bolt for the blade, which may be of galvanised steel, aluminium or bronze. This allows a large rudder area for good handling, extending well below the keel, which can still be readily lifted to the horizontal so it does not project below the keel when at moorings or in shoal water; or may be dropped to a desired intermediate depth when sailing, saving wetted surface, perhaps aiding sail balance, and enabling the boat to

161

be sailed in shallows. The pivot bolt should be carried in small metal cheek plates let into the sides of the cheeks. This bolt support is sometimes incorporated into the straps of the lower rudder pintle, which are swelled out in way of the bolt, which passes through a hole drilled through them.

The rudder blade is raised and lowered by a small-diameter wire lift which passes through a small sheave fitted to one side of the rudder head, leading the wire to a rope tail which belays to a small jam cleat on the tiller. A quick tug on the tail brings the blade up. Care must be taken when making the blade to ensure that it cannot swing so far forward when lowering that it chafes on the after end of the keel.

Small boat rudders are usually hung from the transom, to which the gudgeons are through-bolted. The pintles are usually clench-fastened to the rudder mainpiece but in traditional rudders were often made as a square shank which housed into a square hole in the mainpiece and was set up with a nut and washer drawing it against a shoulder forged or cast on the square shank. More usually the pintles have side straps which are let flush into the faces of the cheeks. Gudgeons and pintles may be of cast iron or bronze, or may be fabricated. Details should be shown on the plans, but if not there are many standard fittings available.

Tillers for small boats are made to suit the owner's fancy; some curved, others straight. They should be slender so that the maximum feel is transmitted from the rudder to the helmsman's hand. The grip need not be thick as a dinghy should be capable of being steered with two fingers in ordinary weather. The tiller should be made to unship from the rudder head on a taper and be secured in place by a pin passing horizontally through head and tiller and being retained on a lanyard.

Finishing

In clinker planking the strakes are almost finished before they are fitted. A properly sharpened scraper is the best finishing tool. This is not the three-sided scraper with a handle but a straight-sided piece of steel, usually sold by the better type of tool stores as a cabinet scraper. Sharpened well it is a true cutting tool which removes a fine shaving and leaves a perfect surface. Alternatively, one can be made from a piece of old saw blade. The edge is ground straight and square on an oilstone, finishing with a few strokes holding it flat, to square the corners. It is then held firmly on the bench or in a vice and any hard steel tool is drawn firmly around the scraper to turn the squared edges. This is done with an up and down motion, about six times, giving an edge which removes fine shavings. An advantage of these scrapers is that they are easier to sharpen, if a nail is caught, than grinding a gapped plane iron.

The ends of the planks and the sides of the stem to the waterline will need to be planed. The ends are fastened with nails which should have been left slightly countersunk below the face of plank. The upper edge of the transom will be rounded off. The stemhead can be cut off to the desired height and shape, usually worked to a curve in traditional open boats or cut off flush in decked craft. It is better to cut all small boat stems off flush with the sheer, in my opinion, as the raised stemhead will do much damage to the topsides of craft the boat lies alongside, and some dinghies have an almost lifelike will in doing this. If cut off flush a rubber fender can be easily fitted to prevent damage.

The boat should be thoroughly glasspapered over inside and out and any stains from paint or glue removed in preparation for varnishing or painting.

Before cleaning rubbish out of the boat it is best to thoroughly clean out the boat-building shop. With all possible waste and dust removed (a vacuum cleaner is ideal for this) the boat may be given a preservative coating. Traditionally this was a coat of linseed oil and paraffin, mixed in proportions of two of paraffin to one of oil. This can be brushed on liberally and will soak well into most timbers forming effective and cheap preservative. Alternatively a modern wood preservative such as Cuprinol may be applied by brush. No varnish or paint should be applied until the preservatives are dry. If the boat is to be varnished inside and out it is common not to apply any preservatives as they may affect the finish of the coating.

The boat can now be removed from the stocks and listed over on one side for caulking the garboard seam and, in larger boats, sometimes the seam of the lower strakes at the stem rebate and at the sternpost, though with good fitting this should be unnecessary.

The garboard seam can be mouthed out or opened with a blunt wooden wedge of hardwood or an iron. On a clinker built boat this needs to be done very carefully. The principle is to get the seam slightly vee-shaped. The number of strands of caulking cotton required must be judged by the width of the seam to be caulked. The strands should be spun together to make a soft rope of cotton which is laid on the seam and gently driven in by looping it. This fills the seam to about half its depth when the looped rope of cotton is hardened home with mallet blows on a fine-edged caulking iron. Caulking is an art in itself and the average home builder cannot be expected to have great skill at it. However, this can be compensated for by care and judgment, plus a little experimenting. The caulking should be driven with equal firmness throughout. If a proper caulking iron cannot be obtained a wedge-shaped piece of hardwood will serve. Alternatively an old putty knife may be ground down to a square blunt edge and used as a caulking iron. A mallet is the traditional tool for hitting the irons but a hammer will serve the non-professional builder.

It should be unnecessary to caulk the plank end rebates at bow and stern, but if it is found to be essential below the waterline to achieve watertightness, this should be done very lightly with one thread of caulking cotton, delicately driven with light taps, or perhaps pressed in. Care must be taken to avoid driving the iron through the thin part of the plank rebates. A caulking wheel may be used for this, if available. These press a thread of caulking home without damaging the edges of a seam or requiring its opening.

The garboard seam and the seams up the stem and sternpost are traditionally stopped, over the caulking or in the bare seam, with a mixture of white lead putty which may be thinned as necessary with a little linseed oil. Its consistency should be fairly firm, like plasticine, as otherwise it will not hold in the seams and draw away from the putty knife. The seams are stopped by pressing the mixture into them with a putty knife and clearing off the excess as work progresses. There are many prepared stoppers available in place of the lead putty and a soft or medium type will be suitable, but probably more expensive.

It is best to paint or varnish the inside of the boat before turning her over. If painted she must be given at least one coat of priming. The commonest paint now used is one of the various metallic-based primers, but purists may wish to use traditional lead paint, which certainly holds tenaciously to new wood for many years, though it may not be compatible with the new paints to be brushed on top of it.

Two coats of flat oil paint should be brushed well on over the primer, rubbing down between coats with fine glasspaper and wiping the dust off afterwards with a clean rag soaked in turpentine. If the coats are thinly applied a fine finish will be obtained for the final gloss coat of enamel.

The inside bottoms of small boats should be painted, over the priming coat, with two thin coats of either red lead or one of the prepared bilge paints such as Danbolin, red or grey. Traditionally, many small boats had the bilge coated with black varnish, which is coal tar thinned with naphtha and often termed 'gasworks enamel', but this is not wise as once timber is so coated it can never be painted without the tar showing through, and as many associate tarred bottoms with an old, leaky boat resale value may be affected.

Varnish must always be applied in several thin coats which will dry quickly and will not run in streaks and blobs. A little chalk dusted over the surface of varnish to be rubbed down will prevent the glasspaper from binding. If an especially fine finish is desired the last but one coat should be rubbed down with a pad and pumice powder, well dampened or better still, with a very fine piece of wet and dry glasspaper.

If possible, it is best to turn small boats bottom up to finish the bottom and sides; supporting the sheer, transom and stem clear of the ground. This makes it easy to finish shaping the keel, stem and sternpost, which may need trimming to a tapered siding and fairing off at the forward and after ends. While upside down the keelband should be fitted, of either galvanised steel or brass flat bar or convex section. If of steel the bar should be drilled and countersunk for the attaching wood screws, before galvanising. It is possible to purchase steel flat bar ready drilled and countersunk at intervals of about 8 in. and galvanised. If this is not of suitable width to protect all the keel siding it may be possible to fit a piece to protect each edge.

A minimum practical thickness for a dinghy keelband is $\frac{3}{16}$ in., to allow for chafe on hards and sand. The forward end must be carried up to meet the half-round section stemband, which may be of galvanised steel or brass, similarly fitted. The after end can be bent around the sternpost heel and carried up the sternpost about 6 in. as protection when grounding or dragging on a hard.

Similar preservative should be applied as for the inside and painting or varnishing carried out. Four coats of natural varnish are a minimum, gently rubbed down with fine glasspaper between coats with the dust wiped off with turps on a rag. This will enable the varnish to permeate the boat's bottom and will help to seal the lands for the first hours of taking up, when the wood swells after launch.

10   Masts, Spars and Oars

Many builders of small boats will prefer to use the excellent aluminium alloy masts and spars which are readily available, but some will prefer to make a golden-varnished spar in keeping with the boat's appearance.

Tools required include rip and crosscut saws, jack plane, mallet, chisels, gouges, calipers and (if available) a hollow bottomed spar-making plane and a draw knife, though these are not essential. Both are unlikely to be possessed by many amateurs but it may be possible to borrow from a boatbuilder. Simple tools may be used as alternatives but will take longer to shape the spar. A drawknife must always be used with care so it does not suddenly split through the wood and cut into the worker's legs or body; also so it does not go too deeply into the wood. Sparmakers have many hollow bottomed planes specially made for shaping various diameters, but the amateur can manage with ordinary trying, jack and smoothing planes, if care is taken.

Wooden masts and spars for small boats are usually of round or rectangular cross section, though they are often tapered in length. They may be of solid or hollow construction. Many designers favour use of rectangular hollow sections with the corners taken off in a small radius.

Solid masts and spars

A solid mast may have a smaller cross sectional area than other shaped masts and therefore generates less windage and leaves less wind-shadow on a sail. Also, a solid mast may be bent considerably. The permissible safe deflection when leeward curvature is controlled by shrouds seems startling to those unaware of its capabilities.

Solid masts may be shaped from a tree in the round, cut from a long baulk of wood, or built up from pieces of wood. A mast

167

shaped from a young tree is usually cheapest. Typically a straight black spruce or fir tree is selected, Norway spruce being a favourite. Both ends of the tree should be examined to locate the heart, which should be as nearly as possible in the centre of the tree at each end. Generally trees of this type have no internal faults, but this can be verified by listening with an ear close to one end of the tree while the other is tapped. The sound should carry with clarity through the spar. The tree should be of slightly larger diameter than the finished mast size. When the bark and sapwood are removed it should approximate to the finished diameter.

When planed and glasspapered to size the spar should be treated immediately with a liberal mixture of one part boiled linseed oil to two parts of paraffin (kerosene) and afterwards stood on end to drain moisture to its heel. Due to greater shrinkage of the outer wood fibres, longitudinal shakes and splits will appear in the surface, but provided the linseed oil/paraffin mixture is applied for some time these should not become serious, and are not a weakness unless of great depth. However, there should be no shakes or flaws across the grain and any knots should be small and firm. Longitudinal shakes should afterwards be filled with a soft mastic stopping which will readily squeeze out when the wood swells. Large knots or flaws should be particularly avoided around the mast wedging position at deck or thwart, and at the gooseneck or boom attachment position.

Grown masts were traditionally used in small craft without shrouds, particularly in Holland and North America. These were stepped with the butt of the tree at the keel to retain the natural resilience of the tree as a mast, helping it to stand without shrouds or stays.

Spruce is the most suitable timber for the masts of small boats to be cut from a baulk, though it is now difficult to obtain in length and will need to be scarphed, care being taken in selection to see that the grain does not distort the completed mast. If a mast or spar is to be made of round section from a square-sectioned piece of wood, which is the simplest method, it should be prepared by being planed on all four sides to within $\frac{1}{16}$ in. of the desired finished diameter. The wood is then converted to an octagonal shape before being rounded. The octagon is marked out by applying a 12 in. rule diagonally across each of the sides, held accurately with the 0 and 12 in. marks at the edges. Marks are made at $3\frac{1}{2}$ in. and $8\frac{1}{2}$ in., at intervals along the wood. There are joined by longitudinal lines and produce the eight sides or panes (87). This may also be done on a spar of diminishing diameter, provided the wood is accurately sawn and planed to the longitudinal taper to suit the varying diameters.

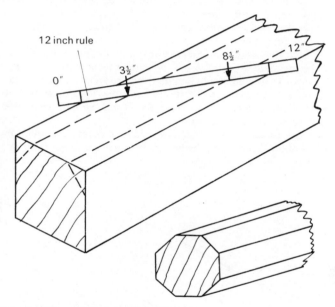

12 inch rule

0"

$3\frac{1}{2}$"

$8\frac{1}{2}$"

12"

87   Marking out mast or spar timber for paning

When planing to round from octagonal, the spar diameter is checked with calipers. Planing marks are removed and the final finish is achieved with glasspaper. It is best to make some templates to the finished diameter of the mast or spar at various points along its length, as necessary. These can be cut from scrap plywood to fit accurately over the radius, and are applied during planing down.

Hollow masts and spars

In a solid mast the core does little to resist the lateral sail load and it may safely be removed; alternatively a mast may be built without a core and the hollow may be of square section.

A simple method of building a hollow mast is from two basic layers of wood joined on the longitudinal centreline with glue. The pieces first have a core of suitable size removed from them by routing out with a power or hand tool. This produces a sound, practical mast (88).

To hold the parts of hollow masts during gluing many cramps will be needed. G cramps are best for the scarph joints, but additional improvised spar cramps for the mast assembly can be made from pairs of bolts of suitable length, nuts and washers, and two pieces of wood (89). These should be applied about every 10 in. along the mast.

Typical construction of a built hollow mast is shown by (90), though the detailed arrangements will be taken from the

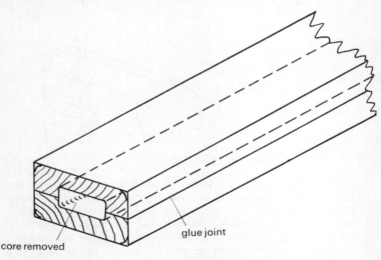

core removed

glue joint

88   Typical construction of a simple hollow mast or boom

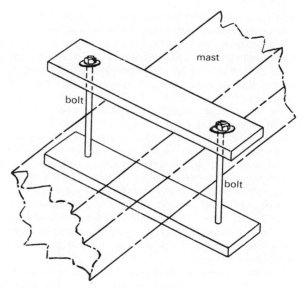

89 Spar cramps

90 Typical construction of simple construction of simple built hollow mast o boom

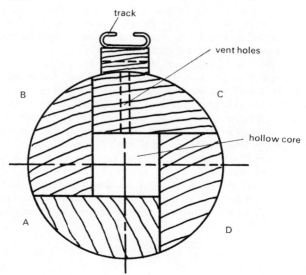

design drawings. To avoid distortion the grain of the component pieces must be arranged as shown in the section.

The design detail scale drawings of the mast or spar may be laid out full size to enable the parts to be marked out easily. To save space they may be drawn out to scale in length but using the full size sections through the mast, positioned at scale intervals.

The lengths of wood available for construction must be known before setting out can be completed, as the four main pieces forming the mast will probably need to be made from other pieces scarphed together and glued. The scarphs must not be less than $4\frac{1}{2}$ times the thickness of the pieces to be joined and must be arranged or shifted well clear of each other so as not to be opposite on the sides of the mast or spar. The amount of shift will depend on the wood available. The use of a sawmill with power tools to cut the side parts will save much time. It will help to mark the component parts of each side piece with coloured chalk for identification throughout construction.

Two faces of each piece must be planed true for fitting and gluing to the others. When working these it is best to wear gloves so that the gluing surfaces are not touched by bare hands as this may inhibit the cure of the glue.

After glasspapering A is wiped over with a clean duster and is laid on a row of horses or in specially made vee-shaped pieces of wood set up in an exactly straight line. B is then glued on and held by as many cramps as possible, spaced about 10 in. apart, taking care to avoid slipping.

When the glue between A and B is set, rotate these pieces through 90 degrees so the long side of B will be resting on the horses. Glue on C and clean out all excess glue accumulated in the trough. Fit and glue any filling pieces at the head, heel, shroud attachments and gooseneck or boom attachment. With the mast still in its 90 degree position, apply the glue carefully to the upturned A shape and then to the two D surfaces before cramping D in place. Time must be allowed for the glue to thoroughly set.

Clean off the glue from the outside seams and scribe the 'box' for making it octagonal prior to shaping it round, as described above. If an allowance of about $\frac{1}{8}$ in. is left all round, when the mast approaches its final dimensions it is best to check for size or diameter with wood templates which can be of $\frac{1}{8}$ in. thick plywood cut out with a fretsaw to final dimensions. Six might be needed in making a typical tapered mast, depending on the number of stations used in marking out. A centreline must be marked in pencil the length of the mast or spar on opposing sides of the diameter, if round, and the templates are applied with centrelines on these lines.

There are more intricate methods of making more sophisticated masts and spars, but these methods will produce a good job, quite suitable for a small boat.

When finished, masts and spars should be either varnished or painted, though many traditional masts were oiled for preservation. About six coats of varnish will be necessary to coat a new mast or spar, being rubbed down between coats. Two coats of priming paint can be followed by two of flat and one of gloss.

Oars

Ash or spruce are the timbers from which oars are usually made, though other woods are used in various parts of the world, sassafrass being an American example. Mahogany and cedar are often used for the wings of oar blades in glued,

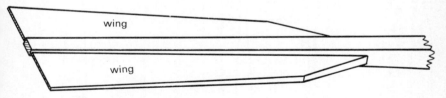

91   Assembly of glued, fabricated oars

fabricated oars. This is now the most common method of oar making. Three pieces of wood are needed for each oar; the long main piece or loom which also incorporates the middle part of the blade, and the wings or side pieces of the blade (91).

173

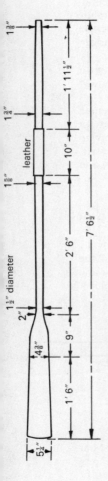

92a Light oar of traditional form of British yachts boats

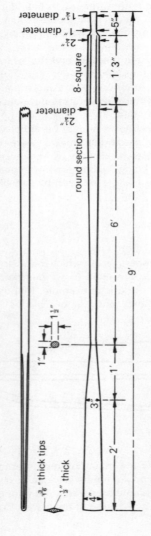

92b Well balanced oar designed by R D Culler

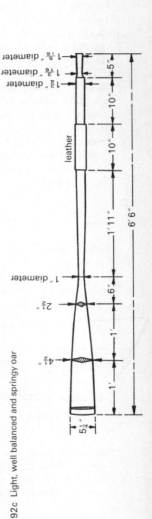

92c Light, well balanced and springy oar

Oars vary greatly in size and type and some typical examples are illustrated (92a–c):

a. A light oar of traditional form much used in yachts' boats of Britain.

b. A well proportioned oar to be made in spruce. The dimensions would need to be slightly reduced if it were made in ash, to maintain the same weight. The oar could be reduced to 7 ft length if proportionally reduced in all dimensions. The eight square looks unusual but puts balancing weight where it is required and was traditional in many parts of the world. The tapered hand grips should be noted as the most comfortable and efficient. These should be left as bare wood, smoothed with glasspaper. The blade section makes the oar almost self-feathering.

c. Some owners like oars with a spring in their length, for pulling, and this is a good example which may be made from ash, sassafrass or clear best-quality spruce. It should be noted that a ridge is carried down the centre of each oar blade, from the neck almost to the tip. The grip is tapered for ease of rowing, an important consideration if one is to row for long periods without getting blistered hands. These oars are well balanced and delicate; they should be carefully treated.

11 Cold-moulded Construction

Cold-moulded construction is ideal for small craft if a smooth hull surface is required for appearance or lying alongside, or if a light boat is needed. It needs methodical care during building but involves little traditional boat-building skill, and was made practical by the development of reliable, waterproof marine glues. Two, three or more layers or skins of veneer or thin plywood are laid over a full sized mould and glued together, being held in place by metal staples or pins until the glue has set. This results in a strong, light hull which can be brought to a fine finish.

Cold-moulding is a more expensive method of boatbuilding than clinker planking, but more complex hull shapes can be built. An important use for it is in making wood plugs from which the reinforced plastic moulds are taken for moulding numbers of reinforced plastic hulls. Cold-moulding affords accuracy of shape for this, besides producing a usable hull after the plastic mould is lifted from it.

It is most desirable that the cold-moulded boat be built bottom upwards to facilitate the fitting and gluing of the skins.

The mould must be accurately made as it irrevocably determines the shape and fairness of the hull. It must be made firm and is usually constructed as (93). True sections of the hull shape are made as moulds, as described in Chapter 2 for clinker building. The centreline assembly of hog, keel, stem, apron, sternpost and stern knee is constructed generally as described in Chapter 3. The transom (if any), hog, sternpost and apron with a stern knee are the basic centreline members which must be fitted into the mould for this type of construction. The hog is usually laminated in place, from two pieces of perhaps $\frac{1}{2}$ in. thick mahogany, screwed to the moulds and glued together. The planking may be run across the hog until it is all fitted, when the lower (actual) face is planed off level and of sufficient width for a keel to be fitted, screwed and glued down to it. Alternatively, a rebate may be formed by the keel being fitted

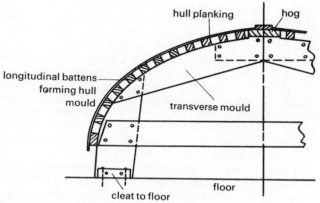

hull planking   hog

longitudinal battens
forming hull
mould

transverse mould

floor

cleat to floor

93   Typical mould arrangements for cold-moulded construction

first to the underside of the hog. A 1 in. wide faying surface
should be wide enough for small dinghies. The stem may be
fitted to the apron after planking is complete, allowing the plank
ends to be run past the rebate line, to be cut off afterwards.

It is important that the face of the transverse moulds be
accurately made to the shape of the inner thickness of the hull
planking, less the thickness of longitudinal ribbands or battens,
which are bent around and fastened to the mould faces and on
which the planking is laid during moulding. Then the finished
planking face will correspond to the designed lines. If necessary
recesses may also be cut in the section moulds for the gunwale,
chine or other longitudinal stiffening which needs to be incorporated, saving much time and work locating these items in
later stages of construction and completion of the hull. Softwood ribbands are best to ease fairing and to provide a firm
hold for the staples, yet allow them to be easily released. The
mould surface need not be continuous and is usually made with
narrow transverse gaps between the ribbands, to save time
and need for fitting the ribband edges. The surface of the mould
ribbands is planed off to shape and checked for fairness with
chalked battens. If necessary outside templates may be applied
to check shape at mould stations. The completed mould, clear

of the rebates on the centreline, is covered with thin polythene sheet, smoothed and fastened. This prevents glue, which may seep through the joints in veneers, from attaching the hull to the mould.

The planking is cut from veneer or thin plywood; African mahogany or agba being preferred. Shears and a sharp knife are used to cut the thin 'planks' to shape. Whichever wood is used it is vital it has good gluing properties. Typical skin thicknesses are: for prams and small stem dinghies, three skins of 2 mm plywood planking; for a 15 ft dinghy, one skin of 3 mm thickness between two skins each 2 mm thick. For a typical dinghy hull three skins of planking will be fitted.

A 45 degree square made from $\frac{3}{16}$ in. plywood will assist in marking out the planking using the hog rebate as a baseline, or alternatively the centreline of the hog. The square should be applied amidships at first, fitting into the rebate against the side of the keel or lower hog, where it can be temporarily screwed or shored down. The first veneer is carefully cut to a typical parallel 2 in. width and is held around the hull against the 45 degree side of the square. If a rebate is formed the rebate line is marked across the plank which is cut to fit accurately. Glue is applied to the plank and the hog in way of the plank landing and rebate, and the plank end is kept firmly in place by two staples which will hold it until the glue sets.

Commonly used staples in dinghy construction are $\frac{5}{16}$ in. and a robust type of office stapler can be satisfactorily used. Wire staples are similar to those used for paperclips but are much stronger and longer legged. They are best driven by a pneumatic gun, completely through the veneer and into the mould beneath, without being bent over, holding the plank down firmly. A small square piece of scrap plywood or cardboard must be laid on the surface of the plank and the staple driven through this to protect the plank surface, but it may be readily removed with a staple remover or pliers. Steel staples may be used but will have to be withdrawn before the next skin of planking is laid or they will probably corrode and result in local distortion and discolouration of the finished hull. It is possible to obtain bronze staples, which are more costly but may be left in the construction.

The first plank is worked carefully around the shape of the

178

hull, keeping close against the 45 degree square and fastening it to the mould with the minimum number of staples required to keep it down and fair. The plank can overlap at the sheer by any amount as this will be trimmed off afterwards. To avoid having to cut each plank to shape, the alternate planks are laid first and owing to the shape of the boat they may not have parallel edges. A space of 2 in. is allowed between these planks at the widest part. When all are laid the intermediate planks are fitted. These are stapled lightly over the gaps between the first planks and are marked out by scribing a cutting line with a gauge set at 2 in. and run along the edge of the adjacent fixed plank (94). The plank is removed, cut to the lines, numbered from forward or aft and put aside, afterwards being fitted to the hog and stapled down as described for the first plank.

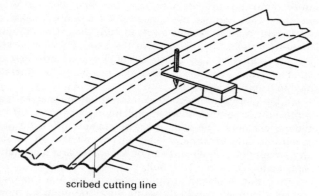

scribed cutting line

94   Method of marking alternate hull planks

If only two skins of planking are fitted there is risk of tiny holes through the glue at the corner crossings of the diagonal plank seams. For this reason it is best to fit a minimum of three skins, which may be laid in sequence: first skin diagonal at 45 degrees; second skin longitudinally; third skin at 45 degrees, in the opposite direction to the first skin. This system will also improve the hull's longitudinal strength. The middle longitudinal skin can properly be made from parallel pieces of veneer, though some shaping will be necessary at the bilge. These need not be the same length as the boat, but only one butt should be allowed in one length of plank and all butts should be well staggered or 'shifted'. The longitudinal skin is more effective in the middle of the sandwich, but if placed outside the planking would need careful marking out and should be of the same length as the boat. Longitudinal external planking will also be wasteful because of the shape.

The second layer of planking is applied in the same way except that each plank is to be glued to the first skin. It is desirable that the seams or edges of the planks are slightly veed on the inside to allow the glue to get between them. When the whole of the second skin has been fitted and lightly stapled in place with washers under the staples, all the planks are numbered before being removed. They are then glued and refitted, removing the staples from the first skin as work progresses. Glue should be applied with a rubber roller, or carefully with a brush, to ensure even spreading. Uneven glue thickness will lead to unfairness in the skin, which will need fairing off, and may also cause air bubbles, which must be avoided or leaks may result. The skin needs to be liberally stapled to help overcome this.

When the glue of the second skin is set, all the staples may be removed with a hook scraper, which will prise them off the protecting washers. The shell must be cleaned off, extra glue removed and any unfairness checked and planed off. A surprising amount of glue weight can be saved by careful cleaning, possibly up to 10 lbs in a 13 ft hull.

The third skin is placed at right angles to the first (opposite 45 degree diagonal) and in the same way, commencing amidships; fitting each alternate plank first, removing it and finally gluing. If the boat is to be varnished, great care should be taken in selecting the timber to achieve matching grain and colour. Ideally all timber for this skin should be cut from the same log and the veneers used in the order of which they were sawn.

After the glue of the outer skin is set the staples are removed and the hull is sanded over to achieve a good finish. The face of the hog is planed flat and made of sufficient width for a keel to be glued and screw fastened to it. This may be made of several laminations, each of perhaps $\frac{1}{4}$ in. or $\frac{3}{8}$ in. thickness, glued and screwed together. If bronze screws are used they need not be removed unless lightness is required. Steel screws can be used if they are removed when the glue has set. The edges of the keel can then be planed to the final shape. When the hull is complete the false stem can be fitted and the sheerline marked from the baseline for sheering down when the hull is turned over.

When removed from the mould the hull will be rather flexible, particularly if the gunwale has not been incorporated on the moulding. It may be necessary to preserve the shape by laying the hull in a temporary cradle of two female moulds, while the inside is cleaned out. It will be found that some glue has squeezed through the joints of the inner skin and will need cleaning off.

Plywood about $\frac{1}{8}$ in. thick is now commonly used instead of veneer. This results in a more rigid skin which does not have the same tendency to distort, but it is more difficult to handle and shape. The transverse moulds needed for plywood planking are the same as for veneer, but only about half the number of longitudinal battens are usually needed due to the greater rigidity of the plywood, which achieves a more constant curve than veneer without closely spaced stapling. A common method of holding the planking is with offcuts of plywood about 1 in. square which have two panel pins driven in on opposite sides. As each plank is glued down it is fastened on the edge to the mould battens by driving in one nail. As the adjacent plank

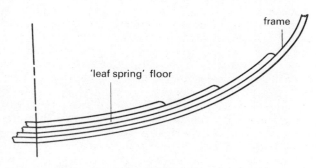

95   Leaf spring frame and floor construction

is glued the other nail is driven into its inner edge so that the seam is held firmly by the lapping washer.

A light, fast dinghy built with three skins of veneer or plywood will not need framing, but in general purpose sailing dinghies it may be desirable to provide two or three transverse frames in way of the mast and shrouds. These can be made in leaf spring form, incorporating floor and frame (95). Having no frames, a cold-moulded hull can be strengthened and protected in the bottom by fitting a layer of plywood inside to form a fixed bottom board taking the chafe of feet.

Appendix 1a

Specification for an 11 ft 6 in. rowing and sailing dinghy

Length overall 11′ 6″. Beam 4′ 8″. Draught of hull 8″. Draught with centreplate lowered 3′ 0″.

Keel. $1\frac{1}{2}''$ moulded by 3″ maximum siding in way of centreplate case. Oak or iroko.

Hog. $\frac{1}{2}''$ moulded by $4\frac{1}{2}''$ sided. Oak or iroko.

Stem. $1\frac{1}{2}''$ sided. Oak crook or lamination.

Apron. $\frac{7}{8}''$ by $3\frac{1}{2}''$ at head, 16″ long. Oak or iroko.

Sternpost (knee). $1\frac{1}{4}''$ sided, $10\frac{1}{2}''$ foot, $3\frac{1}{2}''$ throat, $1\frac{1}{2}''$ head. Oak crook or lamination.

Transom. $\frac{7}{8}''$ mahogany.

Sheerstrake. $\frac{3}{8}''$ mahogany.

Planking. $\frac{5}{16}''$ mahogany.

Garboards. $\frac{3}{8}''$ mahogany.

Bent timbers. $\frac{3}{4}''$ sided by $\frac{7}{16}''$ moulded. Canadian rock elm. Spaced $6\frac{3}{4}''$ centres.

Gunwales. $\frac{3}{4}''$ sided by $1\frac{3}{8}''$ moulded. Canadian rock elm. Open type.

Breasthook. $\frac{7}{8}''$ thick. Arms 11″, throat $3\frac{1}{2}''$. Oak crook or lamination.

Quarter knees. $\frac{7}{8}''$ thick. Arms 10″ on gunwale, 8″ on transom, 3″ throat. Oak crook or lamination.

Thwart knees. $\frac{7}{8}''$ thick, $3\frac{1}{4}''$ throat, $1\frac{1}{8}''$ on gunwale. Oak crook or lamination.

Risings. $\frac{1}{2}''$ sided by 1″. Mahogany.

Bilge stringers. $\frac{1}{2}''$ sided by 1″. Mahogany.

Centre case. Sills 1″. Case sides $\frac{5}{8}''$. Slot $\frac{1}{2}''$. Headledges or stanchions $\frac{1}{2}''$ by $1\frac{1}{2}''$. All iroko or mahogany. Case top capped abaft thwart with $\frac{3}{8}''$ mahogany.

Mast heel chock. Oak or mahogany. Morticed to suit mast heel.

Thwarts. $\frac{7}{8}''$ by $6\frac{1}{2}''$. Mahogany. Single knees.

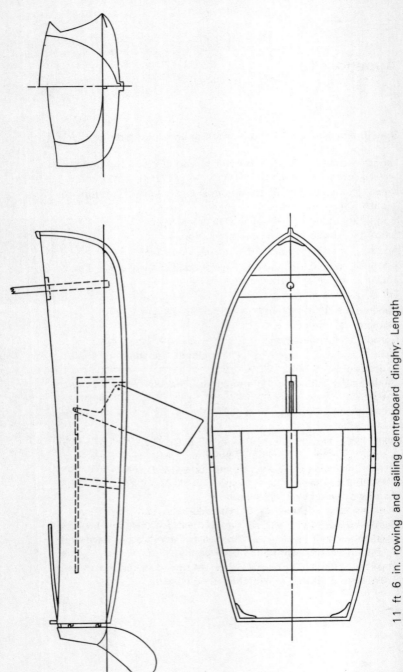

11 ft 6 in. rowing and sailing centreboard dinghy. Length overall 11 ft 6 in., beam 4 ft 8 in.

Rig Bermudan cat or standing lugsail. Sail area 65 sq. ft
Detailed plans to build this boat are available from the author

Side benches. Three mahogany battens, strapped. One port,
  one starboard. Screwed to thwarts with $\frac{1}{4}$" machine screws,
  in cups. One each end, port and starboard.
Shelfing at mast thwart. $\frac{3}{4}$" by $1\frac{3}{4}$". Tapered to $\frac{3}{4}$" at ends.
  Mahogany or Canadian rock elm.
Chainplates. 5" gunmetal or brass. Eyed for lanyards. Port and
  starboard. Positioned $11\frac{1}{2}$" aft of mast centre.
Bottom boards. $\frac{5}{16}$" elm or mahogany. Open type, strapped. To
  lift out in two sections, port and starboard, meeting under
  midship thwart. Secured by $1\frac{1}{4}$" brass turnbuttons to risings
  and to the two middle boards.

Rubbing strakes at sheer. Half-round $\frac{7}{16}''$ by $\frac{7}{8}''$. Mahogany. Fastened with $1\frac{1}{4}''$ by No. 6 bronze screws.

Bilge keels. $\frac{9}{16}''$ by $\frac{3}{4}''$. Oak or Canadian rock helm.

Rudder. Drop type. Blade $\frac{1}{8}''$ galvanised mild steel. Head and cheeks: two $\frac{7}{8}''$ cheeks with $\frac{3}{16}''$ parting piece. Clenched together. Slotted for blade. Fitted with sheave for lifting wire. Morticed for tiller. Blade $23\frac{1}{2}''$ long. Cheeks 18'' long.

Tiller. $1\frac{3}{4}''$ by $1\frac{1}{8}''$, 36'' long, tapered to $1\frac{1}{8}''$ by $\frac{7}{8}''$ grip. $\frac{1}{2}''$ gunmetal jam cleat for lifting pendant.

Centreplate. $\frac{1}{4}''$ galvanised mild steel. Slotted at pivot bolt for lifting out from over pivot bolt.

Pivot bolt. $\frac{1}{2}''$ diameter. Galvanised steel. Set up on washers.

Centreplate lifting arm worked by a rope tackle.

Mooring ringbolt. $\frac{5}{16}''$. Galvanised. Clenched through apron and stem.

Mainsheet horse. $\frac{7}{16}''$ metal rod with end straps to transom.

Other fittings. To owner's choice.

Oars. One pair. Spruce. Varnished.

Mast. Spruce or Columbian pine. To suit sail plan. Varnished finish.

Boom. Spruce or Columbian pine. To suit sail plan. Varnished finish.

Painting and varnishing. Three coats inside and out to owner's requirements.

Rowlocks. One pair galvanised iron. To suit oars.

Anchor. Shifting stock type. 12 lbs weight.

Ancho. rope. 6 fathoms $1\frac{1}{2}''$ circumference nylon.

Stemband. $\frac{3}{8}''$ convex brass.

Sail. Crosscut. Terylene or Dacron. 4 oz. Cut to suit sail plan.

Standing rigging. Forestay and shrouds. Galvanised wire rope $\frac{7}{16}''$ circumference.

Running rigging. Pre-stretched Terylene or Dacron.

Shroud lacings (if used), Terylene or Dacron.

Centreboard hoisting wire. Tackle. $\frac{7}{8}''$ pre-stretched Terylene or Dacron with two $1\frac{7}{8}''$ blocks.

Rudder lift. $\frac{1}{4}''$ circumference galvanised steel wire with Terylene or Dacron tail.

Mainsheet. $\frac{3}{4}''$ circumference pre-stretched Terylene or Dacron. Bow shackle to mainsheet horse and $1\frac{3}{4}''$ block to boom.

Rigging blocks. Wood or plastic with shackles to fittings.

Appendix 1b

Specification for a 15 ft sailing dinghy

Length overall 15′ 0″. Beam 5′ 2″. Draught of hull 8″. Draught with centreplate lowered 3′ 6″.

Keel. $2\frac{3}{8}$″ moulded by 5″ maximum siding in way of centreplate case. Oak or iroko.

Hog. $\frac{5}{8}$″ moulded by $6\frac{1}{2}$″ maximum siding. Oak or iroko.

Stem. $1\frac{3}{4}$″ sided. Oak crook or lamination.

Apron. $1\frac{1}{4}$″ thick. Sided to suit lines. Oak or iroko.

Sternpost. Knee. $1\frac{1}{2}$″ sided. Crook or lamination.

Transom. $\frac{7}{8}$″. Mahogany.

All planking $\frac{3}{8}$″ thick. Mahogany, silver spruce or wych elm. 12 strakes on each side.

Copper land nails placed 3 between each pair of timbers.

Bent timbers. $\frac{3}{4}$″ sided by $\frac{9}{16}$″ moulded, spaced 8″ centres. To be in whole lengths from gunwale to gunwale wherever possible. Canadian rock elm.

Floors. $\frac{7}{8}$″ sided by $1\frac{1}{2}$″ moulded on keel, tapered to moulding of timbers at tips. To have limber holes at the garboards. Oak or laminated iroko.

Gunwales. 1″ sided by $1\frac{1}{2}$″ moulded, tapered to $\frac{3}{4}$″ sided by 1″ moulded at ends. Canadian rock elm.

Breasthook, quarter and thwart knees. $\frac{7}{8}$″ sided. Oak crooks or laminations.

Thwarts. Mast thwart 1″ thick by 8″. Amidships thwart $\frac{3}{4}$″ thick by 8″. Aft thwart $\frac{7}{8}$″ thick by 11″. Mahogany.

Side benches. $\frac{7}{8}$″ thick by $2\frac{1}{2}$″ battens. Mahogany.

Mast thwart clamps. $\frac{3}{4}$″ thick by $2\frac{1}{2}$″. Moulded to fit to planking. Oak.

Risings and bilge stringers. $\frac{1}{2}$″ sided by 2″. Canadian rock elm or mahogany.

Rubbing strake. From $\frac{1}{2}$″ by $\frac{3}{4}$″ mahogany.

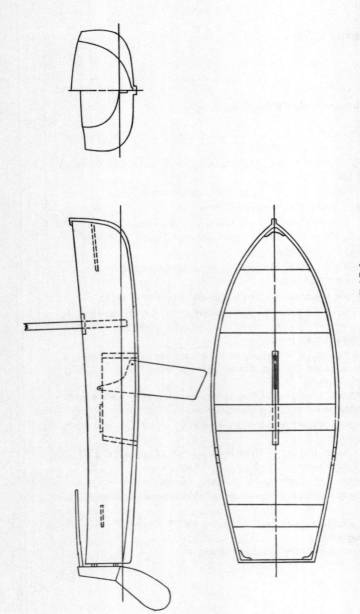

15 ft rowing and sailing centreboard boat Length overall 15 ft, beam 5 ft 2 in.

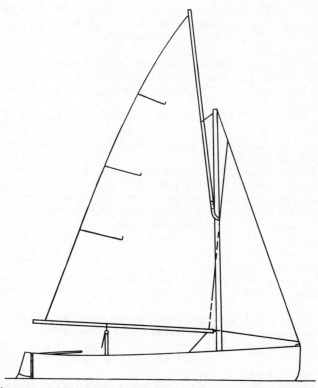

Rig gunter lug sloop. Sail area 132.5 sq. ft. Detailed plans available from the author

Centreplate case. Main pieces 1″ thick, to extend to form mast step. Upper sides $\frac{3}{4}$″ thick. Headledges or stanchions $\frac{1}{2}$″ sided by $1\frac{3}{4}$″, slot $\frac{1}{2}$″. Mahogany.

Sill pieces. $\frac{5}{8}$″ by $2\frac{1}{2}$″ to fit over lower ends of timbers, down to hog. To take check plates for a $\frac{5}{8}$″ diameter galvanised steel pivot bolt which should be a hexagon headed bolt with a nut and washers.

Case capping aft of thwart $\frac{3}{8}$″ mahogany. slotted brass plate to take blows of centreplate lift shackle.

Rudder. Wood blade. $\frac{3}{4}''$ thick, $\frac{5}{8}''$ thick cheeks. Blade to be tapered on edges underwater to about $\frac{3}{8}''$. Mahogany.

Tiller. $1\frac{1}{2}''$ by $\frac{7}{8}''$ at rudderhead forward side. Tapered at grip to $1''$ by $\frac{7}{8}''$. Ash.

Bilge keels. $\frac{7}{8}''$ by $\frac{3}{4}''$. About 5' 6" long. Canadian rock elm.

Plank fastenings; timber fastenings; gunwale, risings and stringer fastenings. 13 gauge copper boat nails clenched on rooves.

Floor fastenings. 12 gauge copper boat nails clenched on rooves.

Throats of floors, knees, breasthooks. 11 gauge copper boat nails clenched on rooves.

Centreboard case to be fastened up with 4" by 18 gauge bronze screws, counter bored, about 1" into keel and dowelled over. Spacings about 7" and the fore end closer.

Case sides to be clenched to headledges. Thwart to be screwed to the top of the case with bronze screws.

Keelbands. One each side of the centreplate slot. $\frac{1}{4}''$ by $\frac{3}{4}''$ galvanised steel or brass flat.

Stemband. $\frac{1}{2}''$ convex brass.

Mainsheet horse. $\frac{1}{2}''$ diameter hard brass with shoulders. To be fitted through the quarter knees and set up with nuts and washers.

$\frac{7}{16}''$ diameter large eyed galvanised or bronze bolt to be fitted for hoisting wire of centreplate and to take tack downhaul.

$\frac{3}{8}''$ diameter galvanised ringbolt with 3" diameter ring to be fitted at each end of boat, through stem and sternpost, for mooring ropes.

A suitable gunmetal or bronze fairlead to be fitted on gunwale close to stemhead, with copper plate chafing piece.

Chainplates. 5" long gunmetal or brass with large bow eyes for lanyards or suitable diameter holes for shackle pins.

Centreplate hoisting gear. Galvanised steel wire rope, flexible, $\frac{5}{8}''$ circumference, with shackle to centreplate, rove through 3" diameter block and with thimble eye at after end. A tackle with a two part single blocks, the fore end with becket and aft one with rope strop should be rigged with the fall leading aft to a cleat on the amidship thwart. Cleat say 6" hardwood. Eyeplate through-fastened to aft end of centrecase for shackling the strop block.

Rowlocks, $2\frac{1}{4}''$ galvanised iron with plates.

Oars. One pair 8' or 9' spruce or ash, leathered.

Anchor. Long shank, shifting stock. 14 lbs weight.

8 fathoms 2" circumference nylon rope.

Mast and boom. Silver spruce.

Sails. Terylene or Dacron, to be in accordance with the sail plan.

Appendix 1c

Specification for an 18 ft sailing boat

Length overall 18' 0". Beam 5' 11$\frac{1}{4}$".
Copper fastened, 2 land nails between timbers.
Stem. Sided 2$\frac{1}{4}$". Oak crook or lamination.
Stern knee. Sided 1$\frac{1}{2}$". Do.
Breasthook. Sided 1". Do.
Quarter knees. Sided 1". Do.
Hanging knees under deck in way of mast. Sided $\frac{3}{4}$". Do.
Coaming knees. Sided $\frac{5}{8}$". Do.
Coaming hook knee forward. $\frac{3}{4}$". Do.
Transom $\frac{7}{8}$". Wych elm or mahogany.
Keel. Moulded 2". Oak, elm or iroko.
Hog. Moulded $\frac{5}{8}$". Do.
Hull planking. $\frac{3}{8}$" thickness. Larch, elm or mahogany.
Garboards and sheerstrake.$\frac{7}{16}$". Larch, elm or mahogany.
Risings. Sided $\frac{1}{2}$", moulded 1". Larch or Canadian rock elm.
Bent timbers. Sided $\frac{3}{4}$", moulded $\frac{5}{8}$". Canadian rock elm.
Stringer. Sided $\frac{5}{8}$", moulded 1". Canadian rock elm.
Floors. Sided 1$\frac{1}{8}$", moulded 1$\frac{3}{4}$" over hog. Arm tip moulded $\frac{5}{8}$".
  English oak.
Gunwales. Sided 1$\frac{1}{8}$", moulded 2$\frac{3}{4}$", tapered to $\frac{3}{4}$" by 2". Pine.
Beams. Forward end of cockpit. Sided 1$\frac{1}{8}$", moulded 2$\frac{1}{2}$".
  Pine or larch.
          Aft end of cockpit. Sided 1$\frac{1}{8}$", moulded 2$\frac{1}{4}$". Pine or
            larch.
          Remainder of beams. Sided 1", moulded 2". Pine or
            larch.
All beams tapered $\frac{1}{2}$" at ends.
Half Beams. Sided $\frac{7}{8}$", moulded 1$\frac{1}{2}$". Pine or larch.
Cockpit carlines. Sided 1$\frac{1}{8}$", moulded 2". Pine or larch.
Mast partners. 1$\frac{1}{4}$" by 8". Pine.
Chocks for foresheets, fore tack fitting and rowlock plates. 1"
  by 3". Pine.

192

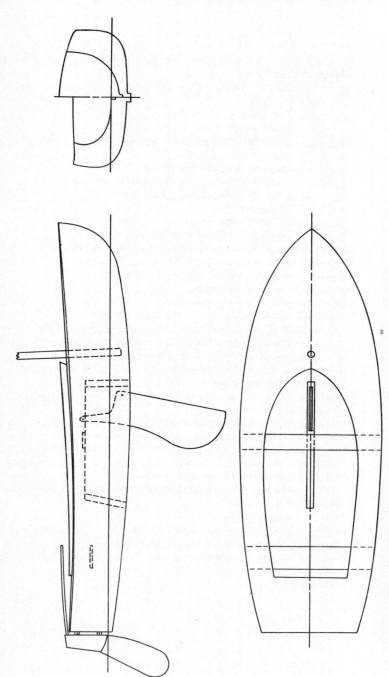

18 ft day sailing centreboard boat. Length overall 18 ft, beam 6 ft

Deck. $\frac{1}{4}''$ thick marine plywood or $\frac{3}{8}''$ thick pine or spruce, canvas covered.

Centrecase. Bottom sides. $1\frac{1}{8}''$ sided by 8". Long screws up through keel. Pine.

        Top sides. $\frac{7}{8}''$ sided. Pine.

        Headledges. Sided $\frac{7}{8}''$. Pine.

        Extension filling pieces forward and aft of headledges. Sided $\frac{7}{8}''$. Pine.

        Capping. $\frac{3}{8}''$ thick mahogany.

        Sheave $\frac{5}{8}''$ with brass plates and clenched pin.

        Sills. $\frac{3}{4}''$ sided by 3". Fitted down over timbers. Mahogany.

        $\frac{3}{4}''$ diameter galvanised steel pivot bolt with bushes. Galvanised and leather washers.

Bottom boards. $\frac{3}{8}''$ thick openwork. Larch or English elm.

Aft thwart. Portable. Sided 1" by 12" wide. Oregon pine.

Forward thwart. Sided $\frac{3}{4}''$ by 8". Oregon pine.

Coamings. Sided $\frac{7}{16}''$. Mahogany.

Rubbing strakes. $\frac{3}{4}''$ by $1\frac{1}{8}''$. Section.

Rudder. Cheeks, two. Sided $1\frac{1}{4}''$. Mahogany or elm.

        Blade. $\frac{3}{16}''$ thick galvanised steel or aluminium alloy. $\frac{1}{2}''$ diameter pivot bolt. Nut clenched after fastening.

        Strong metal fittings for gudgeons and pintles.

Centreplate. $\frac{5}{8}''$ thick steel plate. Galvanised. Slotted over pivot bolt. Edges ground sharp.

Keelbands. 1" by $\frac{3}{8}''$ galvanised steel on each side of centreplate slot. $\frac{3}{8}''$ thick.

Canadian rock elm fitted between them.

Stemband. $\frac{5}{8}''$ by $\frac{1}{4}''$ convex. Brass or galvanised steel.

Chainplates. $\frac{3}{16}''$ thick galvanised steel or bronze. Fitted on hardwood chocks.

Winch for centreplate. To owner's choice.

Tiller. $2\frac{1}{4}''$ wide by $1\frac{1}{2}''$. Oak. Shouldered, fitted with sheave for lift, cleat and retaining pin.

Cleats. To owner's choice.

Mooring arrangements. $\frac{7}{16}''$ diameter galvanised ringbolt in stem. 5" brass fairlead. 12 fathoms $1\frac{1}{2}''$ nylon.

Mainsheet horse. $\frac{1}{2}''$ diameter brass, nutted under quarter knees.

Mast and boom. Hollow silver spruce.

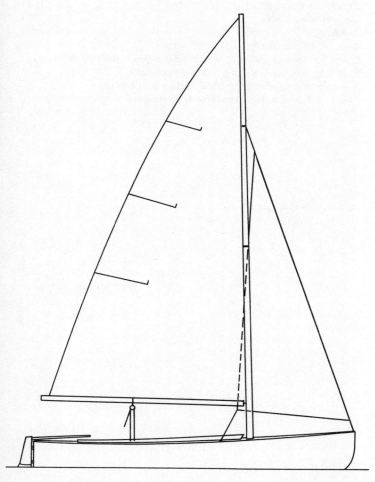

Rig Bermudan sloop. Sail area 198 sq. ft Detailed plans
available from the author

Mast fittings. To owner's choice.
Boom crutch. Oregon pine.
Rowlocks. Galvanised iron. $2\frac{1}{4}''$.
Oars. 9' long. Ash.
Bailer.
Anchor. 15 lbs Danforth or CQR type.
Sails. Terylene or Dacron. In accordance with the sail plan.
Standing rigging. Galvanised steel wire rope.
Running rigging. Pre-stretched Terylene or Dacron.
Painting. Four coats. Alternatively four coats varnish.

Appendix 2

Some woods used in clinker boatbuilding

Acacia, also known as locust A very durable North American wood, also grown in Europe. Light green-yellow in colour with narrow sapwood. Average seasoned weight 40–45 lbs per cu. ft. This wood is little used in Britain but is appreciated in the USA and France. It is equivalent to English oak in strength, and is tough, elastic and finishes well. May be used for keel, hog, bent frames, laminations and other parts of a boat where oak would be suitable.

Apple Although this may seem an unusual inclusion, selected, seasoned apple crooks are used for knees in Britain, Europe and frequently in America.

Silver ash A tough and stringy Australian wood having properties similar to English ash. Used in Australia for bentwood frames and oars. Average weight 43 lbs per cu. ft. Weight range 35–52 lbs per cu. ft.

Port Orford cedar A durable softwood grown along the coast of southern Oregon and California. The grain is of even texture and the wood is a pale pink-brown colour. Seasoned weight is about 29 lbs per cu. ft. It works easily and takes nails and screws well. Used for boat planking and making oars.

Alaska yellow cedar A timber similar to Port Orford cedar with an average seasoned weight of 31 lbs per cu. ft. Can be glued satisfactorily.

Ash, English Weight 45 lbs per cu. ft. The most pliable of English woods. It has a stringy grain which may be hard to plane. If intended for bending it should be selected for straight grain and be grey rather than pink in colour. Ash is not a durable timber and rots quickly in fresh water or if enclosed in a dead air space. It should never be used where rock elm or good bending oak are available.

British Honduras cedar, Central American cedar A durable timber which resembles soft mahogany but is lighter in weight at around 30 lbs per cu. ft seasoned average. Wide range of colour from pale pink-brown to dark red-brown with clear demarcation of sap. Grain is straight but occasionally interlocked. Often used for clinker planking in light dinghies and racing boats. Has a fragrant smell and contains a resin.

White cedar, also called northern white cedar and eastern white cedar A durable Northeastern American softwood ideal for planking small boats. Varies in weight and hardness but is often as light as 21 lbs per cu. ft. There is considerable variation in the seasoned weight of white cedar. The best quality northern white cedar weighs 18 lbs per cu. ft, while New Jersey and Virginia cedar weigh 28 lbs. However, Virginia cedar is not very suitable for clinker planking as it tends to split when nailed and is rather brittle when bent. Pale brown in colour, white cedar is usually available in small dimensions but works well and retains its shape without warping. Durable compared with other light softwoods, it absorbs water easily and must be kept well coated with paint and varnish. White cedar roots were once used as crooks from which to cut grown frames, stems and knees for American small boats.

English elm Usually a tree of the hedgerows but often of superior quality if plantation grown. Although officially classed as a non-durable timber it is extensively used for clinker boat planking, deadwoods and transoms. When seasoned it is of dull brown colour and sapwood is clearly defined. It tends to split and crack when dried out, distorts during seasoning, and must be very carefully placed in stick with closely spaced lines of sticks, vertically spaced, with weights on top of the pile to help reduce distortion. Weight when cut is about 65 lbs per cu. ft, seasoning to about 35 lbs. When cut, patches of pale yellow colour indicate unsoundness. It has confused grain and does not plane easily, often needing dummy scraping to achieve a good finish. It holds nails and screws well. Although it shrinks quickly when a boat is left out of water, it takes up again equally quickly.

English elm is liable to rapid decay if kept in fresh water for more than a few months, and it should never be used to plank boats for continuous fresh-water use. Due to its porous grain it absorbs varnish or paint and requires several more coats than other timbers to achieve a good finish. It can be satisfactorily glued. This timber was much used for clinker hull planking in small working boats in Britain.

Wych elm, also known as Scotch elm and mountain elm This timber is lighter in weight and straighter in grain than English elm. Generally its colour is paler, but often there is little difference between the species. Wych elm is often preferred timber for clinker planking.

Rock elm, also known as Canadian rock elm or cork elm A straight-grained hardwood of eastern America and Canada. Light brown in colour with little distinction between sapwood and sound timber. Average seasoned weight is about 45 lbs per cu. ft, with considerable variation. Tends to distort in seasoning. Has excellent bending properties, being very pliable when steamed. It is extensively used for bent frames, gunwales, rockered keels or other curved members. Rock elm has a tough stringy grain and works moderately well by machine but may tear across the grain with hand tools. It takes nails and screws well and can be glued satisfactorily. Denser grades of white elm may be included in parcels of rock elm, but this is an inferior wood which will probably break when steamed for frames.

Hackmatack, also known as tamarack A North American softwood averaging 38 lbs per cu. ft when seasoned. The roots are much used for crooks from which good stems, breasthooks and knees are made. When seasoned they finish well.

Iroko, also known as kambala A durable hardwood of West and East Africa and the Congo. Usually obtainable in lengths up to 30 ft. It is yellow-brown to dark chocolate in colour, with visibly paler sapwood. When newly cut or planed it is pale, darkening with exposure to the air. The grain is interlocked and sometimes irregular. Iroko has density similar to teak, being about 65 lbs per cu. ft when cut, but reduces to about 45 lbs when fully seasoned. It has been wrongly described as 'African teak' but does not have the natural oil which makes teak valuable for marine work. Iroko can be distinguished from teak by its coarser texture, interlocked grain and its lack of greasy feel and teak's characteristic smell.

Iroko seasons rapidly with usually only slight tendency to split and distort. It is inferior to English oak for bending. If used for keels the edges should be well bevelled or protected with keel bands, as iroko will split and chafe easily on exposed edges. It can be worked fairly easily with most hand tools. When planing, particularly by machine, the grain may cause areas of rough surface which must be finished with a hand scraper. It has good screwing and nailing properties and can be satisfactorily glued. Iroko is commonly used for keels, hog, transom, centreboard case, thwarts, and occasionally clinker planking; although it does not bend to shape easily, has a tendency to split at the rebates and plank ends, and does not swell quickly after launching or being dried out.

Larch, European larch A moderately durable timber commonly grown in Britain and parts of Europe. There are two principal varieties: Scottish and Baltic larch. Straight-grained and resinous, larch often contains many knots and must be carefully selected. It is a tough, stringy wood more difficult to work than spruce or pine but more durable and with greater resistance to chafe and abrasion. Larch shrinks and warps in seasoning and should be used well seasoned, if possible. Seasoned weight averages 37 lbs per cu. ft. Colour varies from white-yellow to red-brown. The paler varieties usually shrink more than the darker. Much used for hull planking in Britain. In some areas larch roots are used for knees. Care must be taken when nailing to avoid splitting, particularly at plank ends and rebates. It needs careful finishing, especially when planed.

American white oak A durable timber grown in the Atlantic and adjacent states of the USA and Canada. Similar to European oak but slightly heavier, it varies in colour from pale yellow-brown to mid-brown, sometimes with a pink tint. Grain structure and weight vary depending on area of growth. Southern white oak is often used for boatbuilding. It is strong with good bending qualities but must be kept from contact with iron or steel, which make it stain. It will glue satisfactorily and usually finishes smoothly with sharp tools, accepting nails and screws well. White oak for bent timbers should not be too dry and may be almost green as the steaming will partly season it.

English oak A tough, very durable timber with a stringy grain which may be difficult to plane if of a distorted form. Average weight 50 lbs per cu. ft. The paler coloured varieties of oak are usually easier to work. English oak warps considerably after cutting, even after seasoning for several years. It has a tendency to split when dried out, though very deep splits will usually close tight after launching. Decay in English oak is often shown by dull red patches. Oak contains acid and will turn black locally where in contact with iron fastenings or if wetted without the protection of paint or varnish.

English oak has been used to build every part of the hull of small and large craft. For small boats it is commonly used for keels, hogs, centreboard case headledges, stem, apron, sternpost and knees. In traditional boatbuilding it was also sometimes used fo clinker planking. Bent frames of English oak were and are often used but require great care in selection, and if the boat to be built has a small bilge radius it is better to use Canadian rock elm. English oak for bent frames should be of young growth cut from near the butt of the tree and used before it is too well seasoned, to take advantage of the remaining spring in the timber. Each oak bent frame should be well steamed before bending. A great advantage of English oak is that it can be obtained with a natural sweep of grain to cut curved members for boatbuilding, such as stems, knees and aprons for small boats. It should never be left in the sun when first cut or it will split, and must not lie on bare ground or it will rot.

Oak was also much used for sawn frames in clinker planked boats, but this practice is obsolete. The natural crook, sawn frame for these craft is much older than the bent timber which became used in England during the eighteenth century and in America by the early nineteenth.

African mahogany Describes a group of moderately durable African woods exported under various names, often those of the port of shipment. In America the wood is usually known as khaya. Average weight is 44 lbs per cu. ft when cut, reducing to 32–37 when seasoned. The yellow-brown sapwood is clearly defined from the good timber which varies from pink-brown to a deep red. It is often marred by gum veins and the grain is usually interlocked. A common defect is thunder shake or cross-fracture; a natural compression failure. Figured logs are more liable to this than plain and the defect is often present in trees which have a soft heart. African mahogany generally seasons very rapidly but occasionally distorts during kiln drying. It cannot be steam-bent but glues satisfactorily and takes screws and nails well. The straight-grained wood finishes well but interlocked grain will probably need finishing with a hand scraper. African mahogany is now widely used for boat planking as it is available in lengths around 30 ft and in wide boards, but it has low resistance to abrasion when used for bottom planking and stains badly in contact with iron or steelwork.

Honduras or Central American mahogany A durable, fine-textured wood, straight-grained and knot-free. Pleasant to work, takes nails and screws well and glues satisfactorily. Compression shakes are sometimes present. Little waste from this timber, which is now most expensive. Average weight 34 lbs per cu. ft seasoned. This wood is not often used for clinker planking due to cost but makes thwarts, centreboard cases and coamings in high class work.

Philippine mahogany Grows in variety; some is hard and dark coloured and some soft and pale. Many boatbuilders do not regard it as a mahogany. Usually it bleaches or turns pale grey with age. Often has interlocked grain and is not strong for its weight. However, the harder varieties make suitable planking provided it is painted. Average seasoned weight 39 lbs per cu. ft.

British Columbian pine A softwood with close, even grain. Stringy, tough and often difficult to work. Average weight 32 lbs per cu. ft. Used for solid masts and spars as it is usually available in reasonable lengths. Less resinous and much lighter than pitch pine and usually free from serious knots. This wood should never be used against oak, which causes it to rot quickly.

White pine (pinus strobus) A durable softwood of North-eastern America averaging 27 lbs per cu. ft weight. Pale straw colour, strong for its weight and durable. Straight-grained, easy to work and stable when seasoned but liable to split. It was once much used for planking yachts' boats, gigs, cutters, etc which needed to be light for pulling.

The state of New York was once covered by forests of this timber and a newspaper advertisement two centuries ago offered a sawmill for sale, adding 'By the mill there is an Inexhaustable quantity of pinewood'. Alas, the lumbermen soon felled the millions of large trees and this wood is scarce. It was also much used in pattern making and for the decks of large yachts.

New Zealand kauri pine, also known as Cowdie pine A moderately durable New Zealand softwood. The straight even grain has a close, even texture. Unlike most softwoods it absorbs little water. It is free from knots, does not splinter and finishes well. Normally purple-grey-brown in colour it may vary to dark red-yellow brown. Seasoned weight averages 36 lbs per cu. ft. Kauri pine is prone to excessive longitudinal shrinkage. It has good nailing and screwing properties and can be satisfactorily glued. This timber is not now usually exported but is used for boat planking in New Zealand, as well as laid decks and other boatbuilding members. It should not be confused with Queensland (Australia) kauri.

Spruce There are several varieties:
Silver spruce. The best known; also called Sitka spruce, Western spruce and tideland spruce. A North American softwood averaging 26 lbs per cu. ft when seasoned. Pink in tone with a marked silver sheen when cut. A favourite wood for planking dinghies. Light, elastic and durable. Has less tendency to split than other spruces. Can sometimes be obtained in wide boards and almost knot-free. Much used for making masts and spars, particularly hollow ones.

Quebec spruce Also called Canadian spruce, St Johns spruce and New Brunswick spruce. Reasonably straight-grained and moderately free from knots. Denser but not so durable as silver spruce. Easy to work and a good planking wood but needs care in fitting to avoid splits.

Norway spruce Also known as Norway fir, white fir and white deal. Weight 32 lbs per cu. ft. Usually has many knots and is liable to cup shakes and splitting. Not a good wood for planking unless very carefully selected. Sometimes used for making grown masts and spars.

Teak A durable hardwood of Southeast Asia. Average seasoned weight 42 lbs per cu. ft. Teak is a handsome wood and anything made from it looks well. It varies in hardness and weight and is filled with a natural oil which prevents water from being absorbed into the grain and consequently it swells and shrinks very little. Although teak is a durable wood its structure is weak and crumbly. It dulls tools quickly and is often filled with minute, hard white specks which may be silicon. Teak is used for thwarts, centreplate cases, transoms and bottom gratings in best quality small boat building.

Utile A durable West and East African wood, open in grain. Of fairly uniform red or purple-brown colour, with light brown sapwood. utile ranges between 34 and 37 lbs per cu. ft seasoned, averaging 41 lbs. It seasons at a moderate rate with a tendency to shakes and some distortion. Working properties are similar to khaya. It glues and holds nails and screws well. Its handsome appearance when varnished makes it suitable for transoms, thwarts and centrecases.

Yacal A Borneo hardwood, straight-grained and with similar properties to oak, being flexible and worm-resistant. Not commonly obtainable except in the East where it is used for bent frames. Average weight 48 lbs per cu. ft.

Appendix 3

Suppliers of small boat building materials and equipment

Timber

Robbins Ltd., Merrywood Mills, Bedminster, Bristol BS3 1DX, UK.
  Tel: 0272 633136
The Maltings Company Inc., 6801 Lakewood Drive, Richmond,
  VA 23229, USA. Tel: 804 285 1096
B. R. E. Lumber, 10741 Carter Road, Traverse City, Michigan 49684,
  USA.
M. L. Condon Company, 260 Ferris Avenue, White Plains, New York
  10603, USA. Tel: 914 946 4111
J. M. B. McCausey, 36329 Harper Avenue, Mt. Clemens, Michigan
  48043, USA. Tel: 313 792 5210
The Harbour Sales Co. Inc., 1401 Russell Street, Baltimore, Maryland
  21230, USA. Tel: 301 727 0106
Hudson Marine Plywoods, P.O. Box 1184, Elkhart, IN 46515, USA.
  Tel: 219 262 3666 (Marine plywood)
Boulter Plywood Corp., 24 Broadway, Somerville, Massachusetts
  02145, USA. Tel: 617 666 1340 (Marine plywood)

Fastenings

Marine Fasteners, P.O. Box 6521, Annapolis, Maryland 21401, USA.
  Tel: 1 800 526 0658 (Bolts and screws)
S. and B. Marine, P.O. Box 6727, Laguna Niguel, CA 92677, USA.
  Tel: 714 956 3760 (Bolts, screws and copper nails)
Robbins Ltd., Merrywood Mills, Bedminster, Bristol, BS3 1DX, UK.
  Tel: 0272 633136 (Bolts, screws and copper nails)
The Copper Nail, P.O. Box 936, Sacramento, CA 95804, USA (Bolts,
  screws and copper nails)
Doc Freemans Inc., 999 North Northlake Way, Seattle, Washington
  98103, USA. Tel: 206 633 1500
STA Fast, 800 Mount Pleasant Street, New Bedford, Massachusetts
  02741, USA. Tel: 617 998 2033
STA Fast, 991 SW 40th Avenue, Fort Lauderdale, Florida 33317, USA
Combwich Marine Enterprises, Combwich, Nr. Bridgewater,
  Somerset, UK. Tel: 0278 652584

Fittings

Davey and Company, 5 Grenade Street, London E14 8HL, UK. Tel:
  01 987 1836 (Rowlocks)

Bronze Star Inc., 1235 Scott Street, San Diego, CA 92196, USA. Tel: 619 226 8500

Spartan, 212 Middleboro Avenue, East Taunton, Massachusetts 02718, USA

Grand River Marine, 38370 Apollo Way, Willoughby, Ohio 44094, USA. Tel: 216 942 3229

South Western Marine Factors Ltd., Pottery Road, Poole, Dorset, UK. Tel: 0202 745414 (Rowlocks)

Simpson Lawrence, 218/228 Edmiston Drive, Glasgow G51 2YT, UK. Tel: 041 427 5331/8 (Rowlocks)

Main Marine Ltd., North Barrack Road, Walmer, Deal, Kent, UK. Tel: 0304 372247

Classic Boat Works, Box 752, Rangeley, ME 04970, USA (Rowlocks – bronze 'Rangeley' pattern)

The Copper Nail, Box 936, Sacramento, CA 95804 0936, USA (Rowlocks – bronze 'Ashbreeze' pattern)

Adhesives

Structural Polymer Systems Inc., 22921 Industrial Drive West, St. Clair Shores, Michigan 48080, USA. Tel: 313 331 8270 (Epoxies)

Gougeon Brothers, P.O. Box 908, Bay City, Michigan 48707, USA. Tel: 517 684 7286 (Epoxies)

Glen L, 9152 Rosecrans, Bellflower, CA 90706, USA

Glossary

Bearding line The line where the inner face of a plank leaves the outer edge of stem, sternpost or deadwoods (the outer edge of the back rebate).

Clench To rivet a nail fastening two or more pieces of timber together. The inner end of the nail is riveted down on a washer known as a roove or rove in Britain and a burr in America.

Fair To make fair. Describes a continuous curve, surface or line without blemish, typically a batten or plank put in place without bumps, hollows or imperfection. Fairing.

Garboard or garboard strake The plank next to the keel. Also known as the sandstrake in Scotland.

Gunwale The longitudinal member strengthening the heads of frames and the sheer of a small boat.

In way of A ship and boatbuilding expression meaning to place a member, fitting or item immediately adjacent to another. To define as being immediately adjacent, i.e. 'lower ends of bent timbers to be fastened to the hog in way of centreboard case sides'.

Land The overlap of two planks which will be nailed and clenched together.

Laying off Setting out the lines, or parts of the lines, and the construction details such as stem, sternpost, centreboard case, etc full size to check the designed lines and arrangements for fairness and accuracy, and to enable full size moulds and templates to be made.

Moulds Accurate, full size transverse section shapes through a hull. Alternatively patterns or parts of the structure which must be made from them. The section moulds are set up on the centreline and clinker planking is made to conform to them to obtain the boat's designed shape.

Offering up To try a member in place to check its fitting to the other structure. To offer up.

Rebate A recess cut in one member to receive another which is carefully fitted to it, i.e. the stem rebate for the ends of hull planking, keel rebate for the garboard plank seam. *Plank end rebate* is cut in the upper and lower edges of the plank ends to allow them to lie flush on each other at the outer surface so they will not protrude beyond the face of the stem or sternpost or transom.

Sare Wood which has dried out and become brittle enough to break when bent within its normal limitations is termed sare.

Scantlings A ship and boatbuilding term for the dimensions of the members of construction. In a small boat usually defined as siding and moulding. Siding means the width or thickness dimension. Moulding is from the implied moulded or shaped surface, usually of varying dimensions, e.g. 'gunwale sided 1 in. moulded 3 in. amidships, tapering to $2\frac{1}{4}$ in. at the ends of boat.'

Scribing If a boatbuilder marks on a member it is termed scribing if done with a pointed instrument or a pencil. e.g. scribing the shape of a knee.

Sheer The sweeping curve of a boat's sheerstrake upper profile. The longitudinal curve of plank lands.

Shore A strut (usually of wood) set up to support or alter the shape of part of a boat or part of its construction.

Spiling If a boatbuilder marks on a piece of timber used as a template or pattern to obtain the shape of a construction member it is termed spiling. E.g. spiling for a plank, spiling board.

Strake A plank which runs the length of a boat's hull.

Sweep The fair curve of a line or a strake of planking.

Through-fastened Describes fastening with nails or bolts which pass completely through two or more members to join them.

Thwarts Transverse horizontal seats fitted for rowing or to step a mast which also tie the hull together transversely. Thwarts are important strength members in small boats.